Love Lette

An Anti

C000245422

Claudiu Murgan
And 33 Fellow Authors

Manor House

Library and Archives Canada Cataloguing in Publication

Title: Love letters to water / Claudiu Murgan.
Names: Murgan, Claudiu, author.

Identifiers: Canadiana 20220429650 |
ISBN 9781988058894 (hardcover) |
ISBN 9781988058887 (softcover)

Subjects: LCSH: Water. | LCSH: Water-supply. |
LCSH: Human ecology.
Classification: LCC GB665 .M87 2022 | DDC 553.7—dc23

First Edition
Cover art: Painting by Sophia Leopold
Edited by Claudiu Murgan
Cover Design-layout / Interior- layout: Michael Davie

158 pages / Approx. 36,700 words.   All rights reserved.
Published November 2022 / Copyright 2022
Manor House Publishing Inc.
452 Cottingham Crescent, Ancaster, ON, L9G 3V6
www.manor-house-publishing.com   (905) 648-4797

I dedicate this anthology to the indigenous peoples from all over the world who, over the millennia, have protected the watery arteries of Gaia, fought against the pollution of the Amazon, and against all odds, are still willing to share their sacred wisdom with those that inflicted incredible pain to their communities.

Acknowledgements

A dream becoming reality is always a worthy cause to celebrate. And this anthology is such an event that will leave its mark on my existence in this timeline, beyond the dissipation of my physical avatar.

I am grateful to all the contributors whose stories shall enchant the readers far and wide. Your gesture will add credits to your generosity bank from which you can withdraw if times get rough. The positive vibe of this anthology springs from our sincere desire to help Gaia sustain and revert the ecological damage we have inflicted, while we are aware that the change within is what embolden us in the first place. I know that we'll make a difference somewhere in the world, and for that reason, I am deeply moved by your solidarity to putting this anthology together.

Special thanks go to Sophia Leopold, the young artist that selflessly donated the front cover illustration. Such talent is rare so early in one's life, so we have to watch her glide to higher peaks of success.

Manor House Publishing, represented by its CEO, Mike Davie, also believed in this project and accepted the proposal. Thank you, Mike and team, for giving this anthology a physical form.

Contents

5

Praise for *Love Letters to Water:*

"I visit Love Letters to Water as a sanctuary. Dipping into its well of wisdom is a long drink and I am deeply nourished and soothed. Water is gentle and strong and inspires me to flow in a natural, life-supporting rhythm. Thank you Claudiu Murgan and all the water worshipers you brought together honoring and celebrating the essence of life..."

- Celeste Yacoboni editor of ***How Do You Pray? Inspiring Responses from Religious Leaders, Spiritual Guides, Healers, Activists & Other Lovers of Humanity***

"This is a very powerful piece of work that brings in so many perspectives for something most souls take for granted. The power of water from not only a life force perspective but a spiritual alignment and a scientific union between the world we live and your own physical body, soul and spirit. Each author brings a different perspective leaving you to want more and reminding each of us of the importance of this precious resource we have been blessed with as humans to survive on this earth. It's a reminder to be in such gratitude for this life force energy! Truly poetic in nature and so divinely put together. A must read!"

- **Tracy L Clark**, author of ***God Where Are you? It's Me!***

Introduction

Water scarcity is a known issue for billions of people around the world and the latest research has predicted that this crisis will only get worse.

Through my own research, I understand that water has memory, water is alive, it could be happy and sad, structured and non-structured. Humanity has lost its way in dealing with nature and especially with its most important element, water.

Since the creation of earth, water and crystals have weaved their paths into a billion-year-long tapestry that has captured the cycles of nature's evolution. It has observed the appearance of humans and their troubled, but fascinating development, and the energies and vibrations of everything that is part of this amazing eco-system.

In the 1990s, being an original thinker, Masaru Emoto, a Japanese scientist, after being introduced to the concept of micro cluster water, had the brilliant idea to freeze water molecules and study them under the microscope. He tried tap water, river water, and lake water, creating in time a pattern of the water quality based on the location of the sample.

He uncovered the fact that water responds to stress, similarly to humans. A molecule collected from a river that flows in a natural setting displays a beautiful hexagonal shape while one from the tap water, which went through the filtration process and kilometers of metal piping, had a twisted and even muddy shape.

After so many years of research, we still haven't unlocked the vast potential of water.

Love Letters to Water, anthology strives to bring forward various points of view and enhance the importance of how we behave vis-à-vis water – and this is further explored in the Foreword by Dr. Gerald Pollack.

All in all, *Love Letters to Water,* anthology gathers a plethora of contributors from shamans to energy healers, from scientists to economists, all showing how significant of a role water plays in their life, spiritual journey, and professional development.

The global importance of water to human life cannot be overstated and it is my hope that you, the reader, will gain further insight into this essential life force via the shared thoughts of our impressive list of expert writers from around the world.

Claudiu Murgan, anthology initiator, primary author, editor and chief contributor, is also the author of three fiction books, two of which are about water. For more, visit: www.ClaudiuMurgan.com

Foreword

Love Letters to Water. What a fitting title for this volume, which contains the works of poets, authors, scientists, shamans, energy healers, and others — each one expressing, in a different way, their devotion to water.

Water has been central to our lives practically forever. From the time of the ancients, it has held both a spiritual and a practical position.

Religious texts of practically all faiths refer to water as having a spiritual essence. The latter became particularly clear to me on a trip to Saudi Arabia, a decade ago. Following my talk, a young Arabic scientist came running up to me with Koran in hand. He had dog-eared the numerous pages where the term "water" appears, and seemed excited to declare the newly discovered phase of water that we has uncovered as the "seat of the human soul."

While his assertion tickled me – by now we know that water can store information as well as various subtle energies — his suggestion that we join together to write a paper on the subject held little attraction for me.

I told him that I had enough trouble in my academic department by espousing something as controversial as a fourth phase of water, and that I did not wish to immerse myself into even more hot water. So, I politely declined.

Over time, I've begun wondering whether he might possibly have identified a critical point.

Where, in fact, *does* the human soul reside?

That incident underlines a lingering difficulty with the common substance that we know as water.

Water sits at the crossroads where spirituality meets science. The two disciplines were once tightly linked to one another, a linkage espoused not only by the ancients but also by many scientists of subsequent eras. Eventually, the two pursuits diverged, running their separate courses.

The separation impacted practically every scientific discipline, including the one where that intersection seemed most evident: water.

In the scientific arena, water had evolved into nothing more than a bland material substance, just like any chemical. The idea that it could be endowed with some kind of spiritual essence largely vanished from the scientific scene.

My sense is that the tide is beginning to turn. With increasingly abundant evidence that water can store information and absorb/emit subtle energies, we are coming to realize that water constitutes a genuine intersection between the physical and the spiritual.

What had been the practically unique purview of the late pioneering spiritualist Dr. Masaru Emoto has become the subject of many scientific studies by prominent scientists. This includes Nobel laureate Luc Montagnier, who studies information transmission to and from water.

At the Annual Conference on the Physics, Chemistry, and Biology of Water, which I help organize each year, the subject of "water memory" has become standard fare. Conferees expect solid scientific presentations on that subject, and, each year they get more and more.

Water has once again become a point of convergence between science and spirituality. That restored convergence is reflected in this volume, which touches on both disciplines and their intersection.

You will find works of spiritualists waxing enthusiastically about the subtle features of water, while at the same time hearing from scientists on their latest findings. The threads weave a kind of integrated fabric that covers the convergence of these two disciplines.

With that in mind, I hope that this volume will provide a meaningful experience for the reader.

Gerald H. Pollack, PhD, Professor, University of Washington

Gerald Pollack is a scientist recognized worldwide as a dynamic speaker and author, whose passion lies in plumbing the depths of natural truths.

He received the 1st Emoto Peace Prize and is a recipient of the University of Washington's highest honor, the Annual Faculty Lecturer Award. He is founding Editor-in-Chief of the research journal WATER and Director of the Institute for Venture Science. Dr. Pollack's (award-winning) books include: *The Fourth Phase of Water* (2013), and *Cells, Gels, and the Engines of Life* (2001).

THE WISH OF WATER

Osei Yaw Akoto (poet), GHANA

How I wish
I live on

How I wish
I remain pure
How I wish
I remain free
How I wish
I remain rich

I'm gas
I'm solid
I'm liquid

I stand
I lie
I flow

I was
I am
And I will

Oh, how I wish
I'm cherished forever
And respected always

How I wish
I remain a friend to all
But enemy to none
Except the one
Who loves to die than to live
How I wish
I remain

Tasteless
Colourless
Odourless

To all people of all times
Oh! How I wish…

Osei's bio:

 **Osei Yaw Akoto** is a Ghanaian born scholar in English Language. He earned a Bachelor's degree in English and Philosophy, and Master of Philosophy and Doctorate in English Language from University of Cape Coast, Cape Coast, Ghana. His PhD thesis was adjudged the Best PhD Thesis in 2018 by the School of Graduate Studies, University of Cape Coast.

Dr. Akoto has published a number of research articles in highly reputable journals, and serves as a reviewer to a number of these journals. Dr. Akoto is an advocate of multilingualism and believes that every language has the right to existence and use.

In recent times, Dr. Akoto has been intrigued by the seminal Shakespearean question, 'What's in a name?'. Hence, he has started projects on personal names, and church names (which remain understudied in the onomastic literature).

In his onomastic enquiries, he adopts approaches such as Systemic Functional Linguistics, Linguistic Landscape Corpus Linguistics, and synergies of approaches to unearth the intricacies in names in Ghana.

Dr. Akoto has built two corporations: Personal Name Ghana Corpus (PNGhana Corpus), and Church Names Ghana Corpus (CNGhana Corpus). He is the founding President of Ghana Names Society.

LOVE LETTER TO WATER

Veda Austin (author), NEW ZEALAND

You and I are intimately intertwined together. Not one thought or dream of mine can escape you, for you flow through every aspect of my experience on Earth.

While in the womb of my mother, you prepared and cushioned my journey into the world, sharing with me the wisdom of my ancestors through the amniotic fluid of memory. As a new baby my eyes saw your varied forms that ever existed in the ethers, before the veil was gently drawn.

I ask, are you me, am I you? All that flows in me is you. My tears are you, my emotions move like waves with you, even upon death you carry the essence of me high into the upper realms of existence. Your form can morph across many worlds, not limited to liquid alone. Perhaps it is you writing these words, moving these hands and in my ignorance I assume we are separate.

You have created an ocean in my heart, and all the moving tributaries are drawn to it and felt through it. Perhaps you take shape and form in all life so that we may find ourselves in all life.

As the creative designer that shapes the world we call Earth, you also shape the body we call I. As I love you, I love me, and I love all. You are my spiritual teacher, my Beloved, my children, my parents, my friends, my ancestors, my loved ones...all bodies of water that you filled with your life force and personality.

Yet why do we feel separate, why do I feel like you are water and I am me when we are in fact the conscious entanglement of one another? Out of the entire casing of the body the eyes are the only visibly liquid organ... is it so that we might recognize ourselves one day as mirrors of one another? As I close the doors of my eyelids, I search inside the rooms of my eyes and see myself as you do, feel myself as you do, and in this place it all makes sense.... the Divine Creation is in motion within me and love is the momentum for flow.

Veda's bio:

Veda is a water researcher, public speaker, mother, artist and author.

She has dedicated the last 8 years observing and photographing the life of water. She believes that water is fluid intelligence, observing itself through every living organism on the planet and in the Universe.

Her primary area of focus is photographing water in its 'state of creation', the space between liquid and ice.

It is through her remarkable crystallographic photos that water reveals its awareness of not only Creation, but thought and intention through imagery.

Veda brings a message of hope and joy from the very source of life itself, she says "Water is transparent, it knows no colour, creed or religion. Water does not judge, nor does it label, it will enter the body of an ant as easily as it will enter the body of a king, or a homeless person or a tree or a dragonfly."

Veda sees water as Source rather than a resource, and considers all bodies of water to be sacred.

Her passion for water extends out of the freezer and into primary schools where she donates time teaching water science and cleverly intertwines it with art projects.

She loves to reconnect children to the living water systems inside and outside of their bodies, believing that the 'tamariki' (children) are the water bearers of the future.

She also spends a lot of time doing interviews and podcasts where she shares her findings and inspiring perspectives.

WATER BRINGS THE BIRDS

Joel Baechle, USA

Water brings the birds. It really does. And countless other things like rodents, insects and all manner of weeds.

But the birds belong. They own the lower atmosphere. They patrol. They manage. They observe. They reconnoiter. They build, they nest and they own. They reside. "Aloft at perch".

If the water departs, the birds notice. They get closer. They approach. They hop along the fence, watching.

But sometimes the water stops, like during a heat wave and a power outage. When the frogs enter the house to survive, the water shortage is real.

Ice melts and the sink becomes a spring, the houseplants an oasis. Then the praying mantises arrive – soon to be headless. They know what love holds in store for them. This does not escape the lizards' notice.

The trees can handle it for a while, even the irrigated ones. But not the garden plants. Two, three days and they wilt noticeably. After five days they are all but dead. Smoke blowing through the aggressively hot air threatens voicelessly. A pungent reminder even in sleep.

The ancient Greeks determined that water was not a mineral because it could be heated to a point of complete invisibility, and condense into its original form without changing.

Water when it comes from the sky has been transported, invisibly at first, then in the form of gathering clouds, until it falls. First it rejoins the earth and extinguishes the fires. Then it fills up the low places and makes puddles again.
Lastly it dampens the soil down far enough that daily irrigation is enough to revive the hopeless vegetation. Full recovery is not

needed for a dried out garden – survival until the next season is enough.

An irrigated garden is a Spring garden. Luxuriant and exotic. Calling with echoes of the French Impressionists. Lavender, rosemary and apricot blossoms. And a pavement of sedum. The steel wire fence prevents a family of deer from marring the illusion.

Water from far away and high above rushes in a flow artesian, dancing over snow-crowned rocks and sun-glint edges, to flow down, down, down and pool deep in the ground where it can be pulled up by energy converted from the sun.

The timers schedule a sufficiency. The bird mother – a female Towhee – shows up shortly before the valves open, and she peeps out a call that quickly draws more to the source. The hummingbirds are first, because they are the quickest and most alert, but also because they live in the garden.

Often bluebirds arrive, followed by finches and sparrows. Others – like the oriole - are more shy and swoop in after the others have gone. Once I pushed two ends of a parted drip line back together, and a tiny fledgling hopped over and drank water by the drop from between my fingers. Trust.

The hummingbirds will fly up close and hover on the edge of a rainbow over an opening bud. Of course, to them it seems farther away and is of no importance compared to the water. You can't reach out and touch a rainbow unless you are the source of the light that is causing it. But once right after a severe hailstorm had left a thick layer of ice balls on the ground the sun shone through the leaves and branches of an oak tree, rising through the clouds like a spotlight, several small rainbows appeared from the water droplets on the oak leaves. I was able to reach out my hand and touch the rainbow because the refracting water droplet was on a nearby branch. Water teaches. Water is a gift.

Water knows the ways of the world. Some people are described as being earthy, but what knows earth better than water, clinging to every crevice and void, always seeking the bottom line? Water knows the depths. Water has been through every plant that's ever grown since there were any to grow, and it knows their ways.

Once a stack of firewood released enough moisture on a glassed-in porch that the water vapor condensed on the windows overnight, and froze into fernlike leaves and fronds, shining and sparking in the brilliant morning sun. Water has a memory.

Water can be held at the triple point under scientific conditions. A sample is placed under a bell jar and the air pressure is reduced towards a vacuum. At the triple point, the water will boil, condense into visible vapor, and freeze into crystals that fall like snow.

Once a dishwasher drain emptied out behind a country kitchen and poured hot water into the snow on a grassy, sunny bank. The vapor rose up into the air like steam, formed a cloud, and drifted into the shade where it froze into crystals and snowed back down on the ground by the drainpipe, continuously. Water remains true to its nature.

Water is powerful. Water flows on ceaselessly until it reaches its goal. If you get caught in an undertow, don't fight it. Swim cross-wise to the current until you get out of it. If you realize that you are "going with the flow" in a rip current, swim across it until you can work your way back in, farther down the shore. Water is a force of nature.

Waterfalls are beautiful when water plays in the air as it passes. But they are slippery and hard. This is the meeting of earth and water. Swimming out to a waterfall looks like fun, but without something to hang onto it will push you away. Falling into rocky channels can be unexpected and lead to disaster. Water provides consequences. Water is honest.

Water can be smooth. "Ripple in still water, with no pebble tossed". Wind can move over the face of the water, and display a romantic shimmer, beneath willow or by moonlight. Or rogue waves can spell tragedy for a sailing vessel, caught by the witch of November on the greatest of lakes.

Sitting indoors on a cold, silver-gray day reminds me that I don't really have to go anywhere.

Midwest by composer Mathias Eck is playing. I need no excuse to resort to fire for comfort – it is lit. The rain is traveling for me – taking me back to the Giant Sequoias and Kings Canyon last year at this time. Some good wine in the John Muir lodge.

Hemmingway spoke of water in his short story, *The Three-Day Blow.*
"Nick and Bill decide to get drunk – very drunk.
Drinking Irish whiskey with water. The way it should be."

Joel's Bio:

Joel was born in Cleveland, Ohio, majored in Sociology, but also edited the college newspaper for two years, while participating in the Stage Band on rhythm guitar. He also took a number of photography and film courses, and had a rock band, which performed a version of the rock opera Tommy with the theater department. Joel played 6 and 12-string guitar.

He often thought that "Sociology" was interpreted by employers as "Socialism", and he soon learned that blue-collar and traditional ethnic groups – Jews, Blacks, Italians, Poles, Cubans, etc. were often kinder to him than the WASP establishment.

For over 30 years, Joel worked in the motion picture special effects industry, while fine tuning his own perception about life, spirituality, and his own purpose in this existence.

His interest in things beyond the normal senses began when he started taking photographs that included images that were not there when I clicked the shutter.

He has been investigating and documenting the paranormal and vestiges of antiquity when he first realized he had taken a photograph on film, of an oak tree dryad on sacred Native American land.

Japanese woodcut waterfall

(photo provided by Fredric Lehrman)

WATER-NESTS

Meera Chakravorty (scholar, poet), INDIA

There are countries that have only deserts,
people there get a few days of rain,
surely not enough though
however much their patience keeps them still!

But once,
they got together to decide,
how to break through the sky to bring rain to their homes,
how the absence of water,
this darkness will vanish from their lives?

After a while,
people saw with amazement
a lot of planes, one after the other
hovering around the sky.
They were pouring salts over the clouds,
which got huge and huge and huge.
Eventually, it rained in their fields,
on their rooftops, on flowers and leaves,
on all the forest groves.

They collected the water to build water-nests
all over the places.
As birds broke into music
peoples' hearts blossomed.
With the darkness vanishing away,
the south-wind brought a strange fragrance.
With gratitude, people looked at the
starry night's vigil,
without the presence of the
wailing wind there.

Water Story

Frayed and stained dusty brown
the woods of California,
in the bondage of a fiery cage,
robbed of elegance.

Days, weeks, months passed ...
people, shut off from its beautiful tangles,
a powerful sovereignty,
a magisterial antiquarian.

In great fear,
people saw the fire spreading like a pandemic,

as if shame was dying before their sight.

They looked at it with regret

and helplessness,

leaving all their burden on earth.

When, after a long spell, it finally rained,

there was water everywhere.

Humans were too frightened

to receive this adornment,

they felt that this gift of water

must not be touched by

unclean hands,

they vowed to accept

this gift offered to them, by sacred love.

Meera's bio:

Meera Chakravorty, PhD. is part of the Research Faculty in the Department of Cultural Studies, Jain University, Bangalore.

Prior to this, she was a professor in Bangalore University from 1975-2009. She has also been a member of the State Women's Commission, Bangalore, Karnataka.

Her engagement has been with Philosophy, Women's Studies, Cultural Studies, Consciousness Studies and Translation projects. She has translated some Award-winning literary works of renowned authors published by Sahitya Akademi (The Academy of Letters), India.

She has been exploring alternative visions and is enriched by both the textual and non-textual sources.

Recent publication: Dynamics of Dissent: Theorizing Movements for Inclusive Futures. Ed. John Clammer, Meera Chakravorty, Marcus Bussey, Tanmayee Banerjee. 2020, Routledge, London, New York. Ed. Chakravorty, Ananthamurthy, Radhakrishna. 2005. Landscape of Matter. Bangalore University, Bangalore.

She was awarded for her writing on 'Time' by University of Interdisciplinary studies, Paris, and John Templeton Foundation jointly. She was also awarded for her literary work by the Tagore Cultural Centre, Bangalore.

Website: www.thirdcitizens.com

(Dr. Masaru Emoto's findings in the molecule of water)

X'IBETH

Howard Charing (shaman, author), UK

Deva of the Water *"Nothing is softer or more flexible than water, yet nothing can resist it."* Lao Tzu.

Here stands X'ibeth, and she is the quintessence of the mysteries of the element of Water. She is a Deva, this is a Sanskrit term meaning 'Shining One', and she is a personification of the spiritual forces that inform the natural world.

She asks you to use your creative imagination, and for a moment, see yourself as a child discovering and playing with the magic of water, and this is not a visualisation exercise, but instead an invitation to engage all your senses in this aesthetic experience.

So close your eyes, take a deep breath and exhale, then recall the sensation of being gently and lovingly caressed with a cascade of warm water. Recall the freshness, the sense of invigoration, the playfulness, the sound of splashing water, the joy and the exhilaration. That child-like innocence is still in you, so why not allow yourself to feel this idyllic sensation?

Recall the times you have been by water, albeit a lake, a river, a waterfall, a sea, an ocean. Hear the soothing sounds of the waves, the gentle wash, the ebb and flow of the tide.

Water is everywhere, not only in the rivers, lakes and oceans, but also in the Earth, the clouds, in plants, animals, and of course within ourselves. Allow the awareness to surface, that we are a river, the water is flowing through us back and forth, a constant toing and froing from the outer world. Water is life, and that the water within us is not ours, we are simply a part of this natural flow. Now X'ibeth suggests that you drink a glass of cool refreshing water, and feel the sensation as it flows into your body.

In this picture, X'ibeth appears as an Oceanide, in one hand holding a golden sceptre, and the other a green-turquoise orb that signifies her dominion over the freshwater sources of the Earth. She is also known as the giant serpent the *Yacumama,* literally 'Mother of the Water' in the Quechua language. In the rich mythology of the Amazon Rainforest, she is the personification of water in its liquid and vapour states that rise to the sky to form rain clouds, an intrinsic part of the bio-ecological cycle for the rainforest and the planet.

The ritual use of water is an integral part of many of the world's religions, as a cleansing and purification, in rivers, ceremonial baths, or as the central sacrament of baptism.

Each year, hundreds of thousands of pilgrims travel to Lourdes to receive healing from the original spring waters in the grotto. Since time immemorial humanity has venerated and blessed the sacredness of water in streams, temples, and natural freshwater sources such as springs.

The four classical elements, Air, Water, Fire and Earth, have a correspondence in spiritual, divinatory, and psychological systems. For example, in astrology, the Zodiac is divided into these four elements, and the Water signs are Cancer, Scorpio and Pisces. The suit of Cups represents Water in the Tarot. Both systems generally describe the characteristics of being centred in the emotions, an orientation towards intuition, and creative potential.

A 'water' person tends to emotionally 'feel' through things. Still, nevertheless, these sophisticated, seasoned, and time-tested divinatory practices that act in effect as mirrors to the soul, demonstrate that the elements need to be in balance with each other. This balancing is similar in approach for traditional healing practices such as Ayurveda, and Acupuncture which work to restore the body's balance, with the primary objective of preventing illness.

The Meaning of this card

If you have drawn this card, X'ibeth proposes that you reflect how the element of water flows in your life. Though this does not mean you were born under a water sign per se, we are composites of all the elements, and at times they may become out of balance with each other.

If the water element is predominant in your life, it indicates that you primarily relate to others and the world via the sense of emotional feeling and intuition. Personal relationships and moral values are essential to you, as, without these, your life lacks a sense of purpose and fulfillment. Just as water will flow into an empty space, so you seek ways to fill an emotional void, this can often happen in intimate personal relationships, to stimulate or perhaps invoke an emotional reaction from your partner.

If life has taught you one thing, and that one thing is, that you must always trust your instinctual (gut) feeling as invariably this is precisely on the mark. In life, this can sometimes be difficult, as in our schools, universities. Indeed, the business world leans far more to the logical, intellectual, and the rational (element of air) domain. Thus these qualities have a higher premium in society's 'value-system' than the ethos of compassion, warm-heartedness, and empathy which you feel that is what our world needs a lot more. In this paradigm, you have learned through many challenging experiences, to flow just like water, and in the words of Lao Tzu, the founder of Taoism, "nothing can resist it".

If you have drawn this card reverse, X'ibeth reminds you that the nature of the water element is flow and that if the flow becomes blocked, it stagnates and loses its vitality and freshness, so if you become too absorbed in your feelings, you also feel blocked.

During these times, you withdraw deep, even fold into yourself, disconnect, and even retreat from the outside world. You are painfully aware that this withdrawal is neither good for you nor those close to you, as it creates the situation that you drive away and become estranged from those you care most. Such a reaction, makes a difficult situation even worse, as closeness, and emotional connection is the primary sustaining force in your life.

At times such as these, X'ibeth urges you to restore your flow, make this a firm intention, and begin with your physical body. Drink more water, and as you drink, in your mind's eye, see and feel it flowing and revitalising your body, your organs, your muscles, and your limbs. In your creative imagination, bring in the Deva of the Element of Water to support you, this will magnetically charge your intention with additional power.

Make more space in your home, clear out possessions and items that you no longer use or need. Start to unblock your physical environment, as this water energy needs space to flow. Water is movement, rivers flow, ocean waves roll, and swish and even the surface of still waters ripple in the wind. X'ibeth knows that you have the potential not just to be in the flow, but *to be* the flow.

Howard's Bio:

Howard G. Charing, born in London, has lived in the Netherlands, the USA, and Peru. He worked in the computer industry from 1970 to 1991. He quit the industry following an elevator crash in which he suffered serious injuries; a broken neck and severe spinal damage. In this accident he suffered a near-death experience that transformed his life. This accident closed the door to his 'normal' prosaic life, however new doors leading to exploration and adventure opened.

Over the last 25 years he has become acknowledged as an international workshop leader on shamanism, an author and visionary artist.

He has worked with some of the most respected and extraordinary shamans and elders in the
Andes, the Amazon Rainforest, and the Philippines. In 2016, Howard organised the first major conference in East Europe 'Sumiruna Awakenings' dedicated to visionary consciousness. This conference featured luminaries such as Graham Hancock, Dennis McKenna, Jan Kounen, plus many others.

He has co-authored 'Plant Spirit Shamanism' published by Destiny Books (USA), and 'The Ayahuasca Visions of Pablo Amaringo' published by Inner Traditions (USA). His latest book published in 2017 by Destiny Books (USA) is 'The Accidental Shaman'. His forthcoming project is 'The Angels of Infinity' an Oracle Divination book and card set, published by Inner Traditions (USA)
https://shamanism.co.uk/howard-g-charing/

LIVING WATERS & A THIRST FOR WHOLENESS

Dr. Mick Collins (author, therapist, visionary), UK

One of the strongest connections I have to water, other than using it for the daily activities of drinking, cooking or washing, is when I visit *Holy Wells*.

I live near the North Norfolk village of Walsingham, where the Virgin Mary appeared to Lady Richeldis in 1061. Mary revealed a vision of the *Holy House of Nazareth* to Richeldis and instructed her to build a replica of it.

During the construction of the *Holy House* a 'hidden well' was uncovered and the healing waters continue to flow to this day. Walsingham is a quiet peaceful village and its gentle energy contains a spiritual legacy that extends back to Roman times, and possibly beyond. Archaeological evidence has revealed the existence of a Roman temple on the outskirts of the village, where religious figurines of the goddess Minerva were unearthed.

The Romans had a habit of building their temples on the grounds of existing religious sites, and it is highly likely that the Roman temple at Walsingham would have been built on the sacred ground of a local Celtic tribe called the Iceni.

There is clear evidence of such practices happening in Britain, notably in the West Country city of Bath, where the thermal waters that were originally dedicated to the Celtic goddess Sulis were integrated with Minerva after the Roman invasion. The two female deities of Sulis-Minerva are still acknowledged at the ancient Bath Spa today.

Walsingham also has a powerful feminine spiritual lineage, which includes Mary, Minerva and most probably Sulis.

I am always mindful during my regular visits to Walsingham that this sacred land has deep and divine connections that go back thousands of years.

It has always been a powerful place of pilgrimage for me, which I find conducive for prayer, dreaming and contemplation. The healing waters from the *Holy Well* are available when the church is open, and they can also be received as part of a short religious service.

Wells remind us of the hidden source of fresh water that comes to us from underground streams and aquifers, and they are also a potent symbol of our own latent psycho-spiritual resources.

In the classic *Taoist* book of divination, the *I Ching*, Hexagram 48 is *The Well*, and the great psychologist Carl Jung was very aware of how this ancient oracle can be used to help realign people with nature and spirit. Indeed, *Wells* takes us beyond surface concerns and they are a powerful symbol that brings us into a deeper connection with the flow of life's sacred energies.

A good example of this is found in the New Testament story of Jesus who meets a woman at a well and asks her for a drink of the water she has just drawn. Jesus then goes on to tell her about the gift of "living waters" that come from God (John 4: 10). This story is a reminder that we need to quench both our physical and spiritual thirsts.

We can access the *eternal spring* of "living water" through our dreams, visions and prayers, as well as our deep connections to plants, animals and nature as a whole. These psycho-spiritual connections have the potential to awaken us to a dynamic and living mystery.

The best example I have that shows how the sacred energy of "living waters" can bubble up from the *eternal spring* is through a dream I had many years ago, which connects to the *Numen Fontis* (mystical font).

In the dream three priest-monks and a young boy (standing on tiptoes to reach the font) were positioned in a quadrant around the vessel. The young boy was gently pouring sand into the font and suddenly the grains started to move slowly in a circuitous way of their own volition.

Gradually the sand started to coagulate and it transformed into a single droplet of water. The felt-experience in the dream was absolutely blissful and these feelings radiated throughout my whole body, which continued after I woke up.

The dream was a perfect representation of latent transformational potentials being activated, where the young boy (i.e. the part of me that is still developing spiritually) was reaching to connect and participate in a sacred ritual with the priest-monks (who represent spiritual archetypes).

The sand was symbolic of the coarse and 'gritty' life experiences that we all have to deal with, which if approached creatively can lead to a more fluid connection with 'grace' and the numinous.

It is no coincidence that the dream symbolism was organized around a baptismal font, where water is ceremonially blessed for the initiatory rite of connecting to the *eternal spring* and "living waters."
Baptism is a ceremony of immersion, which acknowledges our spiritual potential, and like the Hindu practice of submerging prayerfully into the Ganges it is more than a one-off event. It is a reminder that *Holy* water brings us into a sacred relationship with life as a whole.

For many years I have been making an annual pilgrimage to the *Holy Isle of Avalon* (Glastonbury), where I always take time to visit and drink the waters from the *White Spring* and *Chalice Well*, which is always a revitalising experience.

I always meditate next to the *Chalice Well* and every time I feel a sacred presence that is palpable. *Holy Wells* are potent reminders that water should not be squandered and misused.

However, modern industries continue to consume vast quantities of water, which is resulting in underground aquifers being depleted at an alarming rate across the world. It is an ominous warning that we are living perilously out of balance with the nature.

In the modern world we are so used to turning on a tap and gaining instant access to clean water that we are in danger of taking this sacred resource for granted.

There will undoubtedly come a time in the very near future when water will become much scarcer, due to our misuse of this life-giving element.

However, our relationship to "living waters" from the *eternal spring* can be activated when we take time to drink and bathe at *Holy Wells*, which have the power to refresh and renew us body, mind and soul.

A 'thirst for wholeness' could remind us to do something about the chronic 'spiritual dehydration' that is currently afflicting our species.

If we acknowledge a sacred connection to "living waters" we might be able to reset our relationship to life and save the earth from being parched.

Mick's bio:

 Dr. Mick Collins has had a diverse career since leaving school in 1972 aged 15 years. He has worked as a builder's labourer, infantryman and heavy goods truck driver, as well as travelling and working around the world from 1977-83. He also lived in a Tibetan Buddhist Monastery in the UK between 1983-6.

Mick's personal transformative journey includes working through a spiritual emergency experience. This deep encounter catalyzed his vocation, and inspired him to train as an occupational therapist, which led him to work in an acute mental health setting and in a specialist psychological therapies team.

He also spent nine years training in *Process Oriented Psychology*, incorporating humanistic and transpersonal methods into his therapeutic practice.

He also spent 10 years as a Lecturer and Director of Admissions at the *Faculty of Medicine and Health Sciences, University of East Anglia*, Norwich, UK. He retired from academia in 2015.

Mick is the author of several books: *The Unselfish Spirit: Human Evolution in a Time of Global Crisis* (won 2014 Scientific and Medical Network book prize); *The Visionary Spirit: Awakening to the Imaginal Realm in the Transformocene Age – 2018); The Restorative Spirit: Illumination of Conscience and Soul Progression in a Time of Global Awakening – 2022).*

A sought-after speaker, his interests include self-development, deep transformation and the integration of the 'transpersonal' into everyday life.

He lives in Norwich, UK with his wife Hannah and is a father and grandfather.

WATER

Wade Davis (ethnographer, author, filmmaker), CANADA

We are born of water, a cocoon of comfort in a mother's womb. As infants our bodies are almost exclusively liquid.

Even as adults only a third of our physical being has solidity.

Compress our bones, ligaments and muscle sinew, extract the platelets and cells from our blood, and the rest of us, nearly two-thirds of our weight, stripped clean and rinsed, would flow as easily as a river to the sea.

We live on a water planet. Two atoms of hydrogen bonded to an atom of oxygen, multiplied by the miracle of physics and chemistry are transformed into clouds, rivers and rain.

A droplet in the palm of a hand rolls about, fortified by surface tension, a wall of oxygen atoms. Spilled to the ground, it changes shape to match whatever it touches, yet adheres and bonds to nothing save itself.

The unique physical properties of water alone allow tears to roll down the skin, perspiration to bead in the nape of the neck, menstrual blood to flow.

Breath condenses, soft as mist. Rainwater runs as rivulets through cracks in the clay. Rivers of ice harden and flow. Streams slip away to the sea.

Water can be a crystal matrix, solid as glacial ice, as delicate as a snow flake. It falls from the sky as rain, sleet or hail. It disappears as vapor only to reappear as fog. It pools in great caverns beneath the surface of the world, erupts in geysers, cascades over the highest of escarpments, sweeps as oceans above the tallest of mountain ranges.

Water can shift states, becoming gas, solid or liquid, but its essence can be neither created nor destroyed.

The amount of moisture on the planet does not change through time. The water that slaked the thirst of dinosaurs is the same as that which tumbles to the sea today, the same fluid that has nurtured all sentient life since the dawn of creation.

The sweat from your brow, the urine from your bladder, the very blood in your body will ultimately seep into the ground to become part of the hydrological cycle, the endless and infinite process of evaporation, condensation and precipitation that makes possible all of biological existence.

Water in this sense has no beginning and no end. To slip one's hand into a pool, a lake, or an ocean is to return to the point of origins, to connect across the eons to that primordial moment, impossibly distant in time, when celestial bodies, perhaps frozen comets, collided with the earth and brought the elixir of life to a lonely, barren planet spinning in the velvet void of space.

Wade's bio:

Wade Davis is a writer, photographer, and filmmaker whose work has taken him from the Amazon to Tibet, Africa to Australia, Polynesia to the Arctic.

Explorer-in-Residence at the National Geographic Society from 2000 to 2013, he is currently Professor of Anthropology and the BC Leadership Chair in Cultures and Ecosystems at Risk at the University of British Columbia. Author of 23 books, including *One River, The Wayfinders* and *Into the Silence,* winner of the 2012 Samuel Johnson prize, the top nonfiction prize in the English language, he holds degrees in anthropology and biology and received his Ph.D. in ethnobotany, all from Harvard University.

His many film credits include *Light at the Edge of the World*, an eight-hour documentary series written and produced for the NGS.

Davis, one of 20 Honorary Members of the Explorers Club, is the recipient of 12 honorary degrees, as well as the 2009 Gold Medal from the Royal Canadian Geographical Society, the 2011 Explorers Medal, the 2012 David Fairchild Medal for botanical exploration, the 2015 Centennial Medal of Harvard University, the 2017 Roy Chapman Andrews Society's Distinguished Explorer Award, the 2017 Sir Christopher Ondaatje Medal for Exploration, and the 2018 Mungo Park Medal from the Royal Scottish Geographical Society.

In 2016, he was made a Member of the Order of Canada.

In 2018 he became an Honorary Citizen of Colombia.

His latest book is *Magdalena: River of Dreams*, Knopf, 2020.

Niagara Falls – view of both US and Canadian waterfalls

(photo taken by Claudiu Murgan)

HEALING SPRINGS

Meghan Don (author)**, NEW ZEALAND**

Miriam, you who carried the prophetic seed in your soul
Wandering with your people in the parched lands
Your vision bore forth the truth of the waters
The swirling wisdom beneath the Earth rising as the healing
spring

The people clambered for the quenching of their bodies
Their sight short and thwarted
Their pleas desperate and faithless
Beyond and into the waters is where you gazed
Becoming a soul tenderer

Moses and Aaron did not know this way
Their days filled with proclamations and rites
Anger and rules
But you, feminine visionary, you felt and knew the water
Knelt and tasted its otherworldly sweetness

It revealed itself to you day after day
Your body overflowing with its secrets
Your stride strong and innocently proud
The fear of the people you bathed
in the shade of the oak

You knew your time was coming
to slip back into the Earth

Gathering your feminine ones to you
You opened their hearts to your spirit
And to the name of the water

Your knowing lived on
Dancing and singing through time
Rising and falling at the well
Until one day it rose and no longer fell
The one called Magdalene had come

Bearing grace in her body
Her blood flowed unhindered
The living water remembered
As she emerged from the mikveh
Not cleansed, but alive

She drew the women to her at the well
Speaking words of healing
Caressing them with balm of their inner knowing
Wails of long held pain could be heard in the temples

Meghan's Bio:

Meghan Don is an award-winning author, evolutionary mystic, retreat presenter and spiritual mentor. She has been described as "THE VOICE" in showing humanity how to integrate the feminine aspect in our lives.

Meghan was born in New Zealand, where early on in life she learned to communicate with the spirits of the land and the animals, and was deeply aligned with a Maori Tohunga (Shaman). Her work took her to the United States where she taught at Omega Institute, Esalen Institute, The Sophia Institute, and new-thought churches.

Her books are *Feminine Courage: Remembering Your Voice and Vision Through a Retelling of Our Myths and Inner Stories; Sacred Companions Sacred Community: Reflections with Clare of Assisi;* and *Meditations with Teresa of Avila: A Journey into the Sacred,* which won the Ashton Wylie/New Zealand Book Council Award for best book and author.

Meghan is now back to New Zealand to share the wisdom and magic she gained from her world travels.

https://www.meghandon.life/

Waterfall in the mountains of Cerro Punta,
Chiriquí Province, Panama
(photo taken by Claudiu Murgan)

THE MAN BEHIND THE FALLS *(In the depths of Peru)*

Christopher S. Douglas (screenwriter, editor, author), USA

Tears from the sky rained down on Benito's Peruvian village. His mother lay on a makeshift bed in their one-room hut, writhing in pain. At twelve years old, Benito, now his mother's fulltime career since his father passed, struggled to shield his mother from the rain piercing through the straw roof. His mother fixed her gaze on Benito and held out her hand,

"Son, come to me," she whispered.

Benito inched closer and took his mother's hand.

"Do you know why I named you Benito?"

"No, mother. Why?"

Evita squeezed her son's hand while a lone tear strayed from her eye, "It means blessed. You, Benito, are my blessed son. Don't forget that."

"No, mother," replied Benito.

"I am dying, son. You know this to be true. I do not have long. I need you to journey and seek a man called Alejandro. He takes refuge in the mountains behind the falls. You mustn't be afraid. The time has come for you to be a man, Benito. Many people have failed this journey, but the rewards are nothing short of Godly if you make it. Do you understand?"

"Yes, mother."

"Alejandro is so-called because of its meaning – Defender of mankind and helper. He holds the cure for my survival. Truthfully, I know this to be a legend passed down by my forefathers. I have heard distant stories. To be touched by Alejandro hand's is to be touched by the hand of God himself."

44

Weak and exhausted, Evita pointed to a small wooden box.

"The box, Benito."

He reached across and retrieved the box pausing to study the carved image of a man behind a waterfall. Then passed it to his mother. He observed with fascination as she opened it and pulled out a dirty piece of raw wood paper. She held it out for Benito.

"Take this. You will not find the falls without it. Journey with care and stop for no one. Be mindful of obstacles in your path, and do not be deterred. We have no food. Go to the village keeper, and he will provide for your journey. Tell him Evita sent you, and he will ask no questions."

Benito studied the pain in his mother's eyes. He brushed away tears trailing his cheeks.

"I'm scared, mother. What if I fail?"

"Then you have already failed, Son."

He stared into his mother's eyes with a distant and empty stare, "I don't understand."

Evita choked back a lump in her throat.

"If you believe you will fail, then your journey is doomed. To succeed in your quest, you must first seek the belief that is buried deep within you. Cast aside all doubt. This journey will transcend you – go beyond your limits. Do not be afraid."

Benito lowered his eyes and glanced over the worn map.

"Why do you have this map, mother?"

A flash of sadness crossed her face.

"Many years ago, when your father fell ill, your grandfather attempted to make the same journey you will make. Sadly, he was never seen again. A lone wanderer passing through our village months later stumbled across your grandfather's map during his travels and traded the map with the village keeper for food. The village keeper instantly recognized the map and gave it to its rightful owner – me. Now I pass it on to you. Legend has it that the man behind the falls holds the nectar of life in the palm of his hands. For those who successfully find him, their journey is not in vain."

With a monotone voice, Benito asked, "Why does he live behind the waterfall, mother?"

A light skipped deep into Evita's eyes, "It is believed that waterfalls hold the key to the rebirth of spirit and body. The water contains spiritual cleansing powers. We believe it delivers the sacred value of life with its purification and healing powers. Our ancestors have long understood that water is life itself. It is sacred, Son. Our spirit masters know that to purify our bodies in the purest of waters is to cleanse our very soul. Without water, there is no life. That is why he lives in a cave behind the falls. Water is life, and life must be most prized."

Evita paused while catching her breath. Feeling tired and weak, she pulled the woven blanket over her shoulders and repositioned herself.

"Go now, Son. Believe in your journey, and what you seek you will find."

Benito sat quietly for a moment as he watched his mother drift off into sleep. He leaned forward and placed a kiss on her forehead. He gathered a few mere items, wrapped them in a cloth, tied them to the end of a stick, and made his way to the village keeper.

"Benito!" Greeted the keeper.

Benito clutched hold of the map tightly. The keeper glanced at the paper in the boy's hand, instantly recognizing it, his face glowing.

"I am taking a journey," said Benito. "My mother sent me to you for food, *Señor*." The village keeper said not a word and disappeared out of sight. He returned a short while later with a small package and a donkey.

"This is Carlos," he said. "He will serve you well. Journey with caution, Benito."

"Muchas gracias, Señor," said Benito while the keeper walked back into his hut.

Benito looked at his map and stared at the donkey. His lips curled up, relieved and grateful for his surprise transport.

"I'm gonna call you, *Carlito.*"

The donkey brayed once, snorted, and nodded as if he understood, and that made the boy laugh.

The map led to a village named Namora, some distance from Cajamarca, going North near the border of Ecuador into the Andes Mountain Range. Red pencil encircled various names, tracing a serpentine path with random arrows pointing up a mountain, ending in another circle at the peak.

Andes Mountain Range is the most extensive mountain range in the world for those who don't know it. At the same time, Namora is the twelfth district of Cajamarca and stands 2,750 meters tall, 350 meters above Machupicchu.

Benito mounted the back of his donkey, glanced over the small village down the valley, then at the distant Amazon rainforest. With a sigh, he gently tapped the side of the donkey to begin his journey.

After three hours, the scorching sun disappeared behind the mountains when Benito saw a country well. Leaning in, he embraced the donkey's neck and leaned his face into its mane before dismounting.

"Here's a fresh spring for us. This will keep you fresh and strong."

Benito tied the reins straps on a hitching post, pulled a cauldron full of water from the well, and held it for his friend to drink. From his keep, he pulled half a sandwich and an apple. He craved to bite from the apple first, but his hand stopped midway when he saw the donkey's head turned, gazing at him.

"Oh, here you are, Carlito. This is for you," said the boy, watching how the apple made the donkey happy.

It was still light outside, but the evening seemed less than an hour away. Benito loved to ride his donkey. They were at a good pace when they arrived at a fork in the road. Benito tugged the reins to the left after checking with his map, but the donkey stopped. He tapped his sides, but there's nothing in the world that would make a mule change his mind. He pulled the bridle to the right, and the donkey continued at pace again.

"Unless you know of a better way to get to the waterfall, we will get lost, Carlito."

At a distance appeared a small shack, and the donkey went straight at it, stopping at the front of its gate, which surprised the boy. And what was more surprising is that he started braying until an old woman made her appearance from behind the gate.

"Yes?"

Benito didn't know what to say.

"Don't tell me you need a place to stay for tonight because you came to the right hotel," she said with a wink.

"I am sorry, my donkey stopped, you see..."

"I *see* you are on *top* of the donkey. But if you get off, I'll open the gate for you, and you can both have a place to rest. There's a barn with plenty of hay in it, water, and quietness to sleep. Even some carrots for your friend. You're probably heading for the *El Velo de la Novia*, yes?"

"I don't know what that is," Benito said.

"You don't say... It's the *life-giving* cascade... that no one can get to..."

Silence.

"Well, are you coming in or prefer to sleep in the wild? You know, about a hundred meters back that way, where the main road forks left and right? If you've taken the road to the left, you ought to know that someone was killed by a jaguar, not far from where the road starts. Will *that* change your mind?"

"Oh..., I am so sorry. I didn't want to, but yes... thank you," said the boy.

"I'm Angela Maria Chavez. Welcome to my palace," replied the old woman as she opened the gate, swallowing Benito and his donkey inside it.

"Very nice to meet you. I am Benito. And this is my friend, Carlito," his little hand scraping the donkey's mane. But as he passed the gate, he saw that the old woman barely walked. Her tiny house made of adobe had holes in the roof, her yard was unkempt, a country oven looked as if not cleaned for spans, the vegetable greenhouse stood full of weeds, and a well sitting at the edge of the garden had dirt and bird droppings all around and above its round banks. Few hens and geese were loose in the yard, one drake hissing and chasing the donkey before the old woman drove it away with a broomstick.

With a grieved smile and a sigh, she went on with a broken voice:

"I'm old and very sick. I can't keep it clean. Everything has been decaying since my husband passed."

Benito glanced at the heavens to tell how much daylight was left, and without being asked, he immediately started to work. He fixed the roof, cleaned the house, trimmed the garden, scraped the oven to where it looked like new, cleaned the well, build a small chicken house and a fence for the birds, and also pulled from the well's depths few buckets of ice-cold water, which he placed in empty canisters. After he finished, he went to the stream to wash. When Benito returned, he was surprised to see that dinner was waiting and that Mrs.Chavez was looking much better already.

"This is my way to thank you for your wonderful work. You didn't have to do that..."

49

"Thank you, Mrs. Chavez. It is the least I could do for your generosity," said Benito.

And that impressed the old woman.

That evening they all ate well in front of a well-combed vegetable terrace under a starry sky.

The water from the well made them sleep like newborns.

In the wake of the morning, before leaving, the old woman said,

"I am curious. Why would you want to go to the fall and risk your life? You are too young to be needing that water. This is not for you, is it? Who is it for?"

"My mother is very sick. She is dying. She said the only remedy is in... is in that water," he hesitated. "I only have one mother."

"Take this pouch of food. You will need it. There are carrots in the other bag for your mule, too. And here," she said, rummaging through her front apron, "take this from me: cincuenta Soles. You may need them when you reach the cities. You'll see some things you'll want, I'm sure."

Once outside the gate, she pointed toward the path.

"Don't go back to the fork. Take this road straight out and follow it until you reach Cajamarca. Big town. From there, take the path to Namora. From Namora, it will take you a while to climb the mountain where the waterfall is, but the *burro*, eh..., Carlito, will manage the heights with ease. Yes? Just watch yourself. The trail is full of surprises."

"How can I ever thank you? " Benito said.

"You already did when you told me you're doing it for your mother. Nowadays, children do not care about their parents. You do."

"Thank you very much, Señora. Adios."

She stared at the young boy as he mounted his donkey and waved him good luck.

"Vaya con Dios!"

After three days and three nights, it started raining when Benito entered the Calendín province Cajamarca region, taking the road between Pachachaca and Vigaspampa villages. These names may not tell you much, especially if you've never travelled through them. The road between them is the path to uplands rainforest terrains not seen in any other part of Perú.

Benito took out his map, peaked at it quickly, folded it just as fast, and placed it in his side pouch. The rain drummed on top of his straw hat. His mother gave it to him to protect him from the sun and the rain. It was his father's hat, and it fit him perfectly. He was so proud of it. It furnished him with cool shade, and it gave him extreme significance. He straightened his back, pushed his chest forward as if ready for adventure, and called out to his friend:

"Carlito, see that mountain in front of us?" As if understanding, the donkey snorted once. "That's where we're going."

The entry into the amazon forest showed a brownish, thin, bruised trail. Benito stopped at the lip of the woods. The rain halted under the scorching sun as fast as it started and dried everything around. The air carried the scent of freshness as steam raised from the ground. The boy checked his map and scanned the surroundings. There was another way leading to the mountain, as well, but that was too far south. It was safer, he thought, but to reach it would probably take him hours, and he would waste another day, time he didn't have. The woods looked dense, dark, and misty.

They were on soft ground, and just as he was folding his map, the donkey stopped and refused to go no further. Benito pulled the reins to where he had a good view ahead and warily scanned the lawn with his eyes. Few feet away, a rattling sound revealed the whereabouts of a good size rattlesnake curled up facing them. He was not surprised to see it. Few notes and rudimentary drawings were laid on the bottom corner of his map, among which the rattlesnake. Another was the poisonous bullet ant, which grows up to 1.5 inches, making it one of the most giant ants in the world. The Brazilian wandering spider, triple the size of a tarantula, prayed at night, and if it bit you, you would sleep forever.

"Okay, Carlito. Let's turn around for now. I think I know what to do," said the young boy.

Coming to a small pueblo, he bought a belt knife, a box of matches, a five feet bamboo torch, a rag, and some rope from an old merchant. The trader measured him from top to bottom.

"Where are you heading, son?"

"Why are you asking, *Señor*?"

"Because, if you're going where many people went and never came back, I must warn you not to enter that forest if you want to see your mamma again," said the man.

"*Muy bien. Gracias, Señor.* I *do* want to see my mother again," replied Benito.

The man shook his head and made the sign of the cross, watching the boy leaving. *"Dios sea contigo!"* he muttered.

Benito stopped again at the edge of the village at a small creek before returning to his path. He fed his friend another apple, then started cutting the rag into four pieces with his blade.

He wrapped the donkey's feet in few protecting layers of cloth and fastened them with rope.

Moments later, as they paced toward the jungle, he thought of what he learned in school, and his mind prepared for the worst. The most majestic tropical forest in the world stretches over nine South American countries. It provides over twenty percent of the world's oxygen and is home to millions of plants, insects, serpents, water creatures, and ground animals ever known and unknown to man.

Vipers and jaguars were not Benito's only concern. There are over one hundred and fifty indigenous tribes. Aguaruna tribe lives by the Marañón River—the mainstream source of the Amazon River—a body of water more extensive and rich in life than any other.

The Aguaruna tribe hunt with the blowpipe. They dip the tip of their arrows in curare or dart frog poison, and when darted, the pray dies almost instantly. Both are among the most potent toxins in the world.

As Benito approached the lip of the jungle, he paused one more time to examine the woodlands before him.

"Are you afraid, Carlito?"

The donkey began treading forward, giving Benito more courage.

"Me too. I am not afraid," the boy heard himself say. "Now, *despacio mi hermano*. Walk like you walk on clouds as cats walk and stay on the path."

Moments later, the trail, like a tongue, swallowed them unseen.

Sounds of all kinds surrounded them almost instantly. From a tree, Benito observed a three-toed sloth bending over in their direction, eyes closed as if he was sleeping. As the trail narrowed, the woods seem to join. Ahead everything seemed so dense that the piercing sun rays made all shapes mighty shadows, adding to more uncertainty.

His ears adjusted to the new surroundings just when a monkey scared him with its dares that he instinctively tapped the sides of his donkey. Carlito would not go faster if a thousand carrots were in front of him. The boy reached for his torch as the trail narrowed.

.....

53

A good two hours must have passed before they arrived at a clearing, where the sun welcomed them again. A stream at the foot of the mountain confirmed that his map was accurate. If he could cross it without problems and follow up the trail, he would be at the top in few hours, just before sunset.

Benito scanned the surface, looking for any sign of Piranha since this was a rivulet arm of the Amazon River. He knew that the fish usually attack where the water is lower in the dry season, and food is scarce. Red bellies Piranha barely attack when they are starving. Moreover, the donkey's feet were pretty well wrapped, and the distance from one bank to another was not more than a throw of a stick away.

He swiftly descended and began crossing the current. The water was not deeper than two, three feet.

"Easy, Carlito. No splash, okay?"

They were almost across when Benito saw the first Piranha. His eyes bulged as a small group of carnivores rushed up the stream. *Few more feet*, he thought. By his calculations, he had to hurry, splashes or not. The fish already sensed the donkey's scent traveling down the stream.

"Come on, my friend. Go as fast as you can. Go!" the boy cried, lifting up his legs, holding tight unto the donkey. The donkey jerked his hind feet as the group attacked, reaping through the fabric.

"Come on! *Maldito piraña, hijo de puta.*" The donkey grunted and brayed, jerking forward with all its might, hopping on dry land, his feet filled with blood. The boy jumped off and stared at the donkey's legs. There wasn't even a sign of rag protection. He reached for his *ehaleeo*, tore it to pieces, and bandaged its wounds.

"What have I done to you...," he let out, swallowing his tears.

He grabbed the reins, looked at the height of the mountain in front of him, and started hiking.

.....

The peak's plateau was offering the most beautiful scenery. Ferns, grass, and moss-covered the rocky hills. Benito looked around, halting, examining his map.

A circle with an "x" in it announced the ending of his journey. *It's probably a stone-throw away*, he thought. The sun was four fingers over the horizon. It announced its soon-to-be setting, giving the skies nuances of colors that only poets could describe.

The donkey looked exhausted. From its eyes, a wet trace marked its brownish hide.

"We're almost there, Carlito. Please, be with me." Benito kissed and patted his friend. The bounding between him and his donkey grew so much. He loved Carlito as he loved himself.

After some fifty yards, they arrived at a split in a mountain. He examined his map. *There it is,* he said, *down that hill...*

The noise of falling water struck him with energy.

"You hear that, Carlito?"

They started down between boulders. The sound of the waterfall was so invigorating.

The lower they got into the canyon, the louder the waterfall sounded, and the most abundant the vegetation. Dandelions and wildflowers sprang everywhere. The surroundings started to look like a fairytale place.

Another sharp turn and, *lo...* from the middle of the cleft, there it was— the most enchanting cascade in the form of a bride. She stood as tall as a goddess from childhood storybooks, larger beyond imagination.

Her beautiful veil dress seemed to flutter as water gave it life. At the bottom of her dress, streams formed and a pond of most transparent clarity he ever saw invited tranquility.

Birds unknown to him flew above them, all colors and sizes, some calling in different tongues. It looked as if they stepped into another world.

He led his donkey to the water, and both drank from it until their bellies were full. Then they emerged in it to reinvigorate. The donkey brayed and snorted.

"I guess we're safe to sleep here," the boy said. "Tomorrow, we will find the cave and look for Alejandro."

"You already found me, young man," said a man's voice from behind them.

Benito sprang and turned to see a medium-sized man, auburn skin, long hair, and a beard to fit his cave looks. A colored band around his head and a *poncho* over hemp white pants revealed Alejandro's Native pedigree.

"How do you know my name?"

"My mo..., ahem! My mother gave me this map, *Señor* Alejandro," said the boy, handing the man the map.

Alejandro's gaze slipped off of it, resting on the waterfall as if he was taken back in time.

"Welcome to the Velo de la Novia—The Veil of the Bride cascade, son."

"Before anything, please señor, my *burro* needs help. The piraña reaped through the cloth and bit its legs. If it weren't for Carlito, I could not make it to you."

"So, this is Carlito," Alejandro said, his moustache curling upward to cover a smile. "And you are?"

"Oh, I am Benito," the boy laughed.

"Benito, your friend's feet are fine. Look!"

Benito turned and froze for a moment. His eyebrows went high, and his lower jaw dropped. There were no scars and no sign of bites anywhere on the donkey's feet, making the boy cry with joy. A waft of wind-steered water sprinkled them.

Benito's eyes shifted from Carlito to the waterfall in dismay.

"Yes. I know," said Alejandro. "Let's sit down a moment. See how beautiful she is?"

The boy nodded, listening in disbelief.

Alejandro took a deep breath, and said: "[1]It is said that long, long time ago, there were two lovers who loved each other more than life, despite the rivalry of their families. On the wedding day, the bride's father took a rifle a shot the groom killing him instantly. Still, in her wedding gown, she ran from the wedding into the mountains. She could not take the shock nor bear the grief of losing her beloved. She made a pact with [2]Apu and [3]Pachamama, who turned her into a waterfall so that everyone could appreciate its beauty for all eternity. This waterfall, Benito. People do not know that she is still alive, her perennial living water a breathing proof of eternal life." After a pause, he asked, "so tell me, what brings you here, son?"

---

[1] Paraphrased from Peruvian mythology.

[2] In the ancient religion and mythology of Peru, Ecuador, and Bolivia, an apu (God) is the term used to describe the spirits of mountains and sometimes solitary rocks, typically displaying anthropomorphic features, that protect the local people. The term dates back to the Inca Empire. Source: Wikipedia

[3] Pachamama is a goddess revered by the indigenous peoples of the Andes. In Inca mythology she is an "Earth Mother" type goddess,[1]and a fertility goddess who presides over planting and harvesting, embodies the mountains, and causes earthquakes. Source: Wikipedia

Benito started crying with hiccups.

"My mother is dying. She needs... "

Alejandro's brows united. "Say no more. You cannot travel at night. Tomorrow, at sunrise, I will take you to a shortcut that will get you back faster. I will accompany you until we reach the edge of the town.

From there, you will be free of danger.

.....

Benito knocked and yelled at the gate as loud as he could,

"Sra. Chavez! Angela Maria Chavez!"

When the gate opened, Benito gave the old woman a small vessel with water. Please, drink this," he pleaded. He then took the vessel from her hands and ran to the well, pouring the remaining water into the well.

"Sra. Chavez, every time you will pull your cauldron from your well and drink from it, you will drink LIFE. I must run, now!"

"*Dios mio, eres un milagro,*" she cried, as she noticed that her body felt no more pain.

Have you ever dreamt of running in slow motion? The faster you want to run, the slower you can. That's how Benito felt when rushing back home. Hours seemed like days. He prayed to God for his mother to be alive. He had two more canisters—one for her, one for the village keeper.

That day he arrived at home and entered through the gate was the happiest day of his life. The cats on the veranda rushed and greeted him with exciting meows, poking, and tail-bumping as if knowing he will give them fresh water.

As he opened the door, he ran into his mother's bedroom. Her bed was neatly made. On her nightstand, there was an envelope.

His eyes welled as he let out a cry falling to his knees in agonizing pain. He fell into a fetus position, hands over his head, shouting, *mi mami, mi querida mami...* until the bathroom door opened and Evita, pale as wax, hovered over her son, embracing and kissing him.

"*Gracias Dios*," he yelled, taking her into his arms. "I got your water, mom. I got it. I thought something happened to you. The envelope on your nightstand..."

"Oh, the Village keeper gave me a letter as soon as you left. I didn't open it. It is for you. He passed away two days ago.

Benito opened the envelope and read:

My dear Benito,

I know you will make it back. Keep the donkey if you still have it. Where I go, I will not need it. Take care of your mother.

Adios,

Juan

> [4]"The sky—a vault of hope, and nothing more,
>
> Under which you and me our worlds explore

---

[4] Exanthus's Quatrains by C.S. Douglas

Sometimes in wonder; other times in fear,

Whereby illusions and delusions make decor."

Partial extract from the upcoming novel, *The Man Behind the Fall*, by D.G. Torrens and C.S. Douglas

Christopher's bio:

 Chris S. Douglas is an American Internet entrepreneur, businessman, humanitarian, books publisher, and encyclopedist. Douglas is of Romanian, German, and Scottish origin founder of AUTHORPAEDIA® (The Authors' Encyclopedia)— a.k.a.*" The World's Only Encyclopedia Dedicated To Authors"* and ÆTV® <u>AuthorTV</u> (Authors Television Broadcasting). He is also recognized by his cross-genre style as writer of fiction and non-fiction; poet, translator, screenwriter, playwright, editor, lyricist, and musical composer. He is the producer and host of AUTHORPÆDIA LIVE Show at AuthorTV.

WATER, FROM GENERATION TO GENERATION

Emmanuel Kojo Ennin (poet), GHANA

Water, from generation to generation, creation has been with.

Papa Creator has instilled in creature, without which the creature is out of creation.

Animals and humankind, animate and inanimate proclaim its value through utility.

Boiling edibles, making food ready and cleaning the environment are the visible witness.

Water, from generation to generation, creation is refreshed and renewed.

Mama Earth has received raining, vaporization, raining, whose unbroken cycle gives the unending rhythm of creation. Streams and rivers, wells and springs announce its value through utility.

Quenching thirst, satiating hunger, and washing the clothes Are the visible witness.

Water, from generation to generation, Creation has served humankind.

Ancient Days have given joy from childhood to adulthood, infancy to maturity, without which joyful remembrance is lost in creation.

Playing and swimming, showering and bathing, Pronounce its value through utility.

Running through the rains, hearing shouts of peers, playing at the shore are the visible witness.

Water, from generation to generation, creation has provided for humankind.

Papa Sustainer has given protection, security, well being without which human activities vanish in creation.

Human activities, daily events, and seasons tell of its value through utility.

Determining the activities of the ancient economy, providing nutrition, giving the energy of life are the living witness.

Water, from generation to generation, creation has not denied humankind.

Mother Earth has cried for help, protection and sustenance without which, her dependents disappear in creation.

Modern economy, irresponsible use of land, unhygienic behaviors tarnish its value through utility.

Seeking for wealth in minerals, deforestation, spillage of oil are the visible witness.

Water, from generation to generation, creation has given humankind responsibility.

Modern Day has required obligation, accountability, and concern without which, humankind perish in creation.

Providing shade for its source, taking care and bringing back its ancient colour of snowy are the living witness.

Emmanuel's bio:

 Emmanuel Kojo Ennin Antwi is a Ghanaian and a Senior Lecturer at the Department of Religious Studies, Kwame Nkrumah University of Science and Technology, Kumasi, Ghana.

He is currently the Examinations Officer of the Department. He holds a Certificate in Theological Sciences (Pedu), a Bachelor of Arts in Sociology and the Study of Religions from the University of Ghana, Legon, a Post Graduate Diploma in Education from the University of Cape Coast, a Licentiate in Biblical Theology from the Pontifical Urbaniana University, Rome, a Doctorate in Sacred Theology (Old Testament Literature and Exegesis) from the Albert-Ludwig's University Freiburg, Germany and a Certificate in Theology and Religious Studies from the International Graduate Academy, University of Freiburg.

His area of specialization is Biblical Studies and the courses he teaches include: Biblical Hermeneutics, Old Testament Theology, Old Testament and African Life and Thought, Apocalyptic Literature and the Theology of Paul at the undergraduate and postgraduate levels.

He is currently undertaking research in Bible and Society with focus on the Bible and African Life and Thought.

Ennin is a Contributor to the *Arbeiten zu Text und Sprache im Alten* Testament Series (vol. 95) and he has 20 publications to his credit.

He is a member of Ghana Association of Biblical Exegetes (GABES) and the international Society of Biblical Literature (SBL).

Ennin is an ordained Catholic Priest belonging to the Diocese of Konongo-Mampong. He is the Priest in charge of St Martha Catholic Church, Antoa-Kwabre in the Ashanti-Region of Ghana.

ARABIAN SEA THEOPHANY

Matt Flugger (psychic healer), USA

"Guy was the only son of a New York club promoter. His father lived that 1970s life- cocaine, speed and sex with everyone. I used to visit him at the Chelsea. He liked my feet."

This was my friend C talking. His name actually means 'handsome' and he is proof that naming can shape one's destiny. He is the world's most handsome man. Irish candor and coloring with a smoky latin conspiratorial air. A symmetrical face and regal bearing that hypnotizes everyone he meets.

When I first met him, he walked into a journey in Harlem at four am dressed like an Indian prince. He had silver pointed shoes with curly toes and a feathered brooch anchoring a gold lamé turban on his head. When he presented himself in the kitchen of that establishment he also presented two canvas artillery cases, which, once unlocked and unzipped, were a cornucopia of illegal joy and temptation.

Later that morning we sat outside in the courtyard of a building that was once a Methodist church but suffered a conversion to a tantric dungeon. It was August, and at that sunrise hour we were trading sweat with a city that never really cooled off. C was sitting across from me at a picnic table under a tree that was bent into obscenity. I looked at him and said, "We are going to be best friends. Just letting you know." C regarded me for a beat, turned to his right and kissed a man named Peter on the mouth and returned to look a challenge at me with kohl-ringed eyes.

In my life I have made a habit of collecting people who are extraordinary, unique and rebellious. I'm that kind of magnet. I liked him immediately.

Sometime later, we traveled to India. We were standing in the Arabian Sea at Colva Beach in Goa. Once a key Portuguese port for opium production, Goa had become a seeker's mecca with just the right amount of adventure and comfort for middle class Europeans and Americans who sought wisdom through plants and experiences that were illegal at home. We were seekers like that.

I had never been in the Arabian Sea before that moment. The water seemed to be peppered with gold flakes that moved in gentle trails around my legs.

I was beginning to believe that the rumors of the holographic universe were true and we were standing in a curiosity globe on a bookshelf in a deity's reading room.

There was so much sparkling gold it looked like you could simply scoop up a handful of seawater and buy anything.

The sky seemed bigger here than in New York, and as the sun set in the west the moon was visibly entering in the east. Because of our proximity to the equator, the waxing moon sat evenly on its side, like a smile. In the amber stippling sunset atop the waves, deities were presenting themselves.

Standing there listening to my friend talk about his adventures with the foot fetishist, the Indian tree of divinity made total sense. It became entirely possible to imagine a many handed Mohini languidly offering me a sip of Amrita, which is the elixir of immortality, made of this moment, as she strokes my ear, tells me I am beautiful and plots my death. How does anyone evade this beauty?

"Guy always wanted me to sit on this Georgian fainting couch he had in his living room. He would make this big show of taking off my shoes and socks. He would tell me stories about Studio 54 while he stroked my feet. Sometimes we had vermouth, but I never got drunk. He used to give me clothes from the 54 coatroom, which were amazing, so I was cool with the situation."

There can be moments of perfect harmony in life, and often they are quieter than they are loud. Standing waist deep in the Arabian Sea and swirling my arms in the gentle surf, I was aware that the opening of my irises to welcome the night was in perfect harmonic cadence with the setting of the sun. Occasionally the breeze would bring us moments of laughter from the shore, flecks of music, and cymbal sounds of palm trees applauding the night wind, washing away the efforts of the day so the night would have an appropriate stage for mystery.

C kept with his story: *"Guy's dad was a Mason, so he had access to all of these society galas and he traveled in these elite circles. He developed a fetish for forgery. He showed me all of these letters he swiped from private libraries. He replaced them with documents he had created. He had letters from Abraham Lincoln, JFK and Einstein. He loved getting away with this kind of crime. It was a kink. He had many."*

As darkness fell and the fabric of stars revealed themselves in the elegant procession of the turning world, I became aware that the edges of my body were not definite. By welcoming this moment, I was surrendering to an intrigue that was conspiring to teach me something about veils, about the gossamer line that only barely demarcates subject and object.

I was almost something in-between, an idea that flowed through light like music through structure. I felt more space than solid, like the stars above me, like the gold dust patiently considering me and cleaning me with salt and the memory of species in water that emerged from play and disappeared back into becoming. I looked at C and intended a message to him, something sent along a network of communication that was frequency and synesthesia, like I was beaming a color to him that resonated tonally with a wave structure that held this moment together above the sea while still part of it.

C stopped talking and smiled. The story floated away. In the twilight he was beauty and mischief, pirate and fluid adventurer.

As I listened to the wind and the sea and the burgeoning nightlife dodging the packs of wild dogs that came out of hiding to play on the strand, the space between us came alive. Suddenly there were Portuguese marauders who colonized this land with dominance and religion, and there was a pantheon of deities tuning the air to allow older wisdom to dress us. When you step outside measurable time, affinities are everywhere. Jung called them synchronicities. Happenings in toroid causal overlap. As I listened to the night with my body I could see harmonious mapping between sea and sky. There were galaxies below us and above us the stars flowed in tidal bliss. I became aware that everything is moving, everything is alive. As I see the stars, they see me. We confirm each other. All of this in one breath with a friend in a foreign ocean that held me like a child.

The messages gathered momentum:

We are water and we are sky and we are stars.

We are crime and oblivion and love and loss.

We are a part of everything that would not be happening if we were not there to witness it. We are surrounded by miracles that pass through us and across our field of vision. We are the eyes of god.

And through all of that beauty and wonder and chaos there was one truth that pulsed over and over, one constant, resonant message presented in sound and body waves and currents of energy expressed as light, nostalgia and comfort:

All of these things are gifts.

All of it.

Everything.

Witness the world from this place and all beauty is possible. You have that choice.

All this to continuous applause from the trees.

Matt's bio:

Matt is the host of a travel series called *The Divine Field*, in which he brings a cast of rebels to far-flung corners of the world in pursuit of ancient wisdom. He believes that if we can demonstrate our connection through the relational field and bring people into contact with their divine power, we might just save the world. A seeker of spiritual insight for over twenty years, Matt has travelled the globe, sitting in ceremony, exploring holy sites, and engaging sacred modalities in pursuit of knowledge and experience to support his expanding relationship to divine intelligence.

Matt loves taking the path that is blind to culture and bright to guidance. After business school, Matt attended a prestigious visual arts school by applying with a written transcript. He has performed as a slam poet in Boston, where he also sang light opera. When he was unable to attend the only available film class in his five college area, Matt created a film festival and hosted it instead. Matt's first short film, FIND, was nominated for Oscar competition at the Austin Film Festival.

Matt has always been curious about spirituality. He's crossed the US as an honorary Jew, and later he considered accepting Jesus Christ as his personal savior with the Baptists.

Matt has performed in the US and Canada as front man of the rowdy blues duo The Black Currents and as guitarist with Peter Murphy of goth innovators Bauhaus. Matt enjoyed an award-winning career at Sony Pictures Television, with his creative work reaching an audience of 75 million viewers by the time he left in 2016. Matt enjoys an ebullient curiosity and prefers to be in motion, seeming to prefer destinations where there are motorcycles, guitars and a curiosity chest of fellow intransigents. www.wearespiritwalker.com

TEARS OF THE MOTHER

Dr. Kylie P. Harris (author), AUSTRALIA

In Melbourne, Australia, it is raining.

My son asks me, "Where does the rain come from Mummy?"

I tell him, "Mother Nature is crying baby".

He asks curiously, "Why is she crying Mummy?"

I tell him, "Sometimes she cries when she's happy and sometimes she cries when she's sad. It's our job to make sure she cries tears of happiness".

And then I walk away and cry.

Because I worry that one day the Mother may stop crying.

And my son may stop being curious.

And the mothers of the world can feel my worry.

Somewhere else in the world, it is flooding.

A son asks his mother, "When will the rain stop Mummy?" She tells him, "Soon baby".

Her little boy shivers. "I'm cold Mummy".

She tells him, "You'll be dry soon baby".

And then she walks away and cries.

Because her little boy is cold and wet and she fears that the Mother is crying too much.

And her son may never be dry again.

And the mothers of the world can feel her fear.

Somewhere else in the world, it has not rained in a long while. A son asks his mother, "When will the rain come Mummy?" She tells him, "Soon baby".

Her little boy cries. "I'm thirsty Mummy". She tells him, "You will drink soon baby".

And then she walks away and cries.

Because she has no water for her little boy and she wonders if the Mother will cry again.

Or if her son will drink again.

And the mothers of the world can feel her anguish.

And the mothers of the world cry her tears.

For they are the tears of the Mother.

And the mother knows, as all the mothers of the world know, that our sons may lose their curiosity, and they may get cold and wet in the tears of the Mother.

But if the tears of the Mother dry up, then the whole world will be crying.

Kylie's bio:

Kylie P. Harris, PhD, is an independent research psychologist, writer, and activist from Australia. She is an academic at the University of New England, and a research assistant for The Juice Media.

Her doctoral thesis investigated the relationships between spiritual emergence(y), psychosis, and personality.

She has presented her work at local and international conferences, and published book chapters and journal articles in peer reviewed journals.

Kylie is a founding board director of The Australian Centre for Consciousness Studies, a member of the Emergent Phenomenology Research Consortium, and an Ambassador for the WallOBooks and Great Life Choice programs.

She works experientially and her research is guided by personal experience. She is interested in investigating the psychology of climate change and the global crisis; and shamanic and Indigenous perspectives towards healing and transformation.

She also enjoys writing and presenting for the general population, including radio and podcast interviews for mainstream audiences.

Entering the sacred site of the Heitate shrine, Japan
(photo provided by Michiko Hayashi)

LOVE LETTER FROM WATER

Michiko Hayashi (Ambassador and Global Director of the Emoto Peace Project), JAPAN

LOVE and GRATITUDE from the heart of Water to your heart. I am Water, and I am life.

I am love, and I am the catalyst of all vibrations.

I am love because I give life to all beings. When I am frozen in the cold temperature, the ice floats so that all the living creatures in the water can stay alive.

Every droplet of water merge as one and it flows in harmony with nature and never fight with each other. I am usually peaceful, calm and gentle when the environment is so, but when humans are very disrespectful for nature and me, I give rough warnings and it is also my love for the humanity even though it may not seem it is to humans.

Sometimes I experience hardship as waterfalls, and when I'm shocked, I wake up, am revitalized, and become energetic water. I help seeds to sprout and give powerful energy to breakthrough soils and even asphalts so the sprouts can grow. It is my love for all plants.

I rise in the trees against gravity so that every corner of branches and leaves of the trees stay well and alive because I love them unconditionally.

It's sad to see people say "oh, it's raining." I wish they would see me as "blessing rain." Humans are the only ones out of all living beings who complain about rain. And when they complain, their vibration attacks me and I become broken heart. Children are excited when it rains and have fun playing in the rain and I become happy because I feel their joyful vibration.

We live our lives mostly as water. The essence of a human being as well as all living beings is WATER.

"All existing things have vibrations, or Hado. This energy is often positive or negative and is easily transmitted to other existing things. Hado is integrally woven into the implications of water's response to information." Quote from THE TRUE POWER OF WATER by Masaru Emoto.

Water circulates by transmitting information (energy = Hado) and connecting lives. The movements of water reflect the spiral energy of our consciousness and affect all lives of living creatures. As water touches soils, it receives the trace minerals' information as well as transferring such information.

We are all made to live in water and live to connect with everything through water. Water IS the connection of all things and beings, thus if water becomes very pure and clean, the whole world will be pure and peaceful. Water shows that the combined two words together, "Love and Gratitude" makes the most beautiful crystal. It implies that the creator must have designed this whole earth based on love and gratitude.

What do you think is the most essential energy necessary for sustaining human life? My answer is love and gratitude. The most important form of energy that we have on this earth is the ability to love someone wholly and purely and to be filled with gratitude when you are rescued from the edge of despair.

Love is the energy that we give to others, and gratitude is the love that we receive from others. So, the greatest form of energy results from the harmony between the energy of giving and the energy of receiving. This energy is absorbed and carried by water as the conductor.

With the energy of love and gratitude, water can be healed and thus it can heal us. However, as it is a conductor of our energy; emotions, thoughts, words, etc, negative and destructive energy can affect all beings and all things on this earth.

In the Japanese mythology there is the Shinto god of water called SUIJIN. It refers to the heavenly and earthly manifestations of the benevolent Shinto divinity of water and is widely found in rivers, ponds, lakes, wells, and springs. It's also called Ryujin which is the Japanese dragon god related to water.

Many people believe that Shinto water god is the guardian of fishermen and patron saint of fertility, motherhood, and painless childbirth. We also worship water god with offerings, believing that it will ensure pure and unpolluted water for drinking, agriculture, and sanitation.

Many people dedicated water god stone markers at dikes, agricultural canals, rice paddy fields, mountain springs, regular springs, streams, wells, rivers, and even inside sewage water and septic tanks. When water god stone markers are enshrined at mountain springs, they become sources for agricultural waterways, and they will associate with the mountain gods.

Many Japanese festivals are dedicated to the water god, and they occur mostly in summer and winter. Those observances have a significant role in the exorcism of bad spirits and purification. They are mainly done to avoid dangerous epidemics, diseases and natural and man-made water-related disasters.

Sacred water of shrines that we obtain and take crystals form very beautiful as if water god is revealing his existence in it.

Knowing that we are water ourselves, we can always purify ourselves by offering benevolent thoughts, love and gratitude to water. This is the most effective way to heal any water energetically. What we shall always remember is purity of our heart when we offer our prayers because water is the mirror of our mind, thoughts, and spirits.

It may be very interesting for many people to learn that there are more than 400 names to differentiate rains in Japan.

In the category of "heavy rain", names differ depending on the size of water drops, how intensive the rain is, how long or short the intensive rain lasts, whether the rain is poking like a thin bamboo, etc. In case of tender rain, names differ whether they are short and gentle, is it sparsely dripping rain, or is it fine rain like fog?

Or, if the rain is not so heavy and continues to fall, or has it been raining since last night, or does it continue to rain for many days, etc.

There are names for blessing rains and rains that describe different colors, or interesting rains such as rain that moisturizes specific persons, rain for lovers, as well as different names of waters in different seasons.

We are very blessed that we are abundant in rain and water, but if we did not have the culture to appreciate water, we may have not had blessings of water.

From ancient time, it seems that we were aware that all of our benevolent prayers and emotions were transmitted to water and water gods who provide us abundance, safety and protection.

We shall never forget this beautiful culture and always respect, appreciate and take care of water all around us, and of course water within us.

If each "I" remember it and appreciate water, the whole world will have abundance in beautiful pure water and harmony in the world, and that is my sincere hope.

Michiko's bio:

 Michiko was born in Japan, where her father was a chief Buddhist priest. She learned to be humble, honest, diligent, and compassionate from who he was. She has a B.A. from a university in the USA with foreign language major (fluent in Japanese, English and Spanish). Between March, 2004 and October 2014, she worked as an administrative personal assistant to Dr. Masaru Emoto until his transition in 2014. He was the founder of the Emoto Peace Project, the pioneer of HADO (vibration), researcher of water, and author of world best-seller "The Message from Water", "The Hidden Messages in Water", etc.

Michiko shares the importance of living positively, kindly and with respect based on love and gratitude through "The Message from Water" to make the world a harmonious and peaceful place. The children's book "The Message from Water" has been translated into 34 languages. www.EmotoPeaceProject.net

Sacred Water of the Heitate shrine, Japan

(photo provided by Michiko Hayashi)

LOVE LETTERS TO WATER

Rainey Marie Highley (author, coach, yoga teacher), USA

Inside...

> You have journeyed with us.

> For eons. Unnoticed. Unrecognized.

Finally.

Our conscious union begins...

> We sing.

> You move.

> > *Masaru Emoto taught me that.*

> Sacred geometric dancing...

> Creates the energetic conditions.

Alchemical Transmutation.

> Trans-form

> > Frozen

> > > now melting

> > Liquid

> > > evaporating

> Mist in between

> > Steam

> > > *It's all moving, you see.*

> > Plasma

> > > *You read about the 4th phase, right?*

> > What is that, you say?

> Liquid Light

> That's right

We ascend.

Transcend.

Trans-form

The human condition a distant dream...

Memories flooding back.

Respect, reverence, realization

Your sacrifice etched forever...

Engraved in every molecule,

Imprinted on our souls...

Love

and

Gratitude

Always

Love

and

Gratitude.

Rainey's Bio:

Rainey Marie Highley is an award-winning metaphysical author of over seven published books including two #1 Amazon bestsellers and the award-winning book, *The Water Code: Unlocking the Truth Within.* As a Spiritual Life Coach, Soul Tribe Teacher & Guide, Rainey helps clients shed societal programming, accelerate their spiritual growth, awaken to their soul's mission, and grow in happiness, confidence, strength, and courage. Rainey is based in Sedona, Arizona USA. For more, go to www.4authenticity.com.

RIVER

Darcie Friesen Hossack (poet), CANADA

we walked along the riverbed turned over the bleached bones of
washed down trees

ideas we had when I thought I knew you

seed heads of anemones picked up with wind- swept sand that

scours our eyes until

scales fall away

we used to talk on the swing on your porch

while hummingbirds perched to

 sit and

sip nectar from a jar

we are the hands and the feet you said, and picked up a stone

to throw in the river,

where it rippled the surface and sank

you offered me dates from the bank of

another place, where

people have been replaced by trees

Darcie's bio:

Darcie Friesen Hossack is an author and poet from the edge of Jasper National Park in Alberta, Canada. Her short story collection, *Mennonites Don't Dance stories*, was shortlisted for the Commonwealth Writers' Prize and runner up for the Danuta Gleed Award. She is the Managing Editor of WordCity Monthly, a global online literary journal dedicated to themes of diversity and peace-building, and she has lately completed a novel called *Stillwater*, where, for a family with a Mennonite mother and a Seventh-day Adventist father, the End Times are just around the corner.

Katori Shrine, Japan
(photo provided by Michiko Hayashi)

SEALSKIN

Emmi Itäranta (author), FINLAND

When the song reaches my ears, the water awaits, wide and unpredictable as life.

I slide into it from my rock, chasing the tide, and it encloses me: a weightless space scattered with stars as sunlight catches on floating speckles of sand.

I swim towards the voices through a woods of undulating stalks where slow-moving sounds and muted outlines wrap around each other.

Here I live as I am meant to. In such temperatures frail human shells would slow down and stiffen, stop moving in minutes. Yet my dense fur and the layer of fat underneath keep me warm and smooth as a stone in a hot spring.

From the sounds I can sense the direction in which the singers gather, and where the prey: shoals of fish with flashing sides, scrambling every which way as I approach.

The song binds me and pulls me closer. The spindle-shaped shadows float together as a herd, making music that carries across the surface, climbing the crests and dipping again. The song weaves and webs and clusters, calling me. I shift my strong tail, swim faster and reach them, the soft outlines of the singers, and join in.

My head breaks through to the daylight and breeze. My voice catches the thread-end of theirs, knots it into something new. One of them nudges my belly, another gives my flipper a curious lick.

The eldest circles me several times, then stops upright underwater, her nose towards the light, blowing air bubbles: *You may come along. You are kin, even if you are something of a stranger.* When I am certain they will not try to attack me or drive me out, I dance through the waters with them.

81

The currents of the sea sing against my skin; within, I move freely, and together we make our own music, wild and unchained.

But there is only so far I can go until the land calls for my return. While the others carry their song with them towards the open sea, an invisible cord I cannot sever catches me and pulls me back to my rock: a free-floating plant that would leave its deep-buried roots, then starve with nothing to nourish it.

Against the wide-carved waves I swim back.

As soon as I jump to the dry land I become heavy again. The way up is long, my body a slippery boulder that wishes to roll and slide and return into the space of water.

The setting sun has shed its glow on the rock, its coarse warmth a comfort and renunciation at once.

With great effort I make my way to the small crevice where I left my disguise. With my teeth I grasp it, pulling it towards me. It looks empty and frail without my flesh to fill it, lifeless as a mask.

Clumsily I manoeuvre myself into the skin, put on the face and limbs and hair.

I stand naked on the cliff, cold in the evening breeze. I wonder if in other dark and narrow places on this islet or others I might find more skins: hidden, perhaps, or else abandoned for good. I wonder if any of them might wear faces I know: of the grey-haired lady behind the till at the convenience store, of the young assistant at the harbor pharmacy, of the person I fall asleep holding at night.

Perhaps they too come here sometimes, when the human skin becomes too tight and uncomfortable to live in.

Perhaps they cast off their shells and return to the water we all came from.

The song still carries from the sea.

In order to survive in the world, I walk home, away from home.

Emmi's bio:

Emmi Itäranta was born in Tampere, Finland, where she also grew up. She holds one MA in Drama and Theatre Studies from the University of Tampere, and another from the University of Kent, UK, where she began writing her debut novel *Memory of Water* as a part of her Creative Writing masters degree.

Itäranta has also published two other novels, *The Weaver* (US title) / *The City of Woven Streets* (UK title) and *Kuunpäivän kirjeet* (*Moonday Letters*).

The awards given to her books include Kalevi Jäntti Prize, Young Aleksis Kivi Prize, Kuvastaja Award and Tampere City Literary Award. Itäranta's professional background is an eclectic blend of writing-related jobs. She lives in Canterbury, UK, and continues to write fiction in two languages. http://www.emmiitaranta.com

The Pacific Ocean washing the black sands at the Coronado Beach, Panama.
(photo taken by Claudiu Murgan)

83

NAMING CEREMONIES FOR EVOLUTIONARIES

Carol Kilby (ritualist of evolutionary spirituality), CANADA

Foreword

Baptized as an infant into the Christian culture, I eventually was ordained and carried on the tradition of marking children with holy water, "in the name of the Father, the Son, and the Holy Spirit..." The intent being that the baptized would follow Jesus's ways and know the promise of eternal life.

Today rising and polluted waters are evidence of the planet's crisis. The world needs new rituals that bring focus to the divinity of life on Earth and a new culture of Evolutionaries. The intent of an Evolutionary Ritual is to name a new human species that is consciously evolving in this time and to initiate them into a culture of human-Earth mutuality that promises a sustainable future.

Carol Kilby. Evolutionary Dancer, Out, In, and On the Fringe of the Church

Preparation:

Location: Outside - near a stream, brook, lake, river, ocean. Large, beautiful bowl. 3 pitchers to carry water from source to bowl. Evergreen branch.

Or, Inside – table-top fountain in which water runs over rocks. 3 pitchers of water. Evergreen branch.

Readers

RL= Evolutionary Ritual Leader

WB = 3 water bearers

E = those taking the name Evolutionaries

Gathering

Music, Drums, Earth flags.

Teach first verse from the Creation Spirituality Chant.

CSC Theme Weave

Netti Garnr

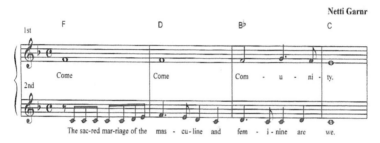

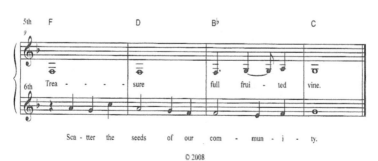

© 2008

Naming the Sacred intention:

RL. Dancing with our grief for the ecological crisis, our longings for a culture of human-Earth mutuality, and our potential to be cocreators of that future, we come to name those among us who today commit to consciously becoming *Evolutionaries.*

Celebrating the Sacred Intention:

All chant: Come, come, comm-unity! *Drums, whistles, clapping, stomping.*

Honouring the Evolutionary Moment:

RL. To mark thresholds in the journey of life – birth, adolescence, death – humans in every time and place have created rites of passage. But here and now, we must create a ceremony to mark our–species' evolution on the passage from its Anthropocene to Ecozoic age. With lamentation, we leave behind a stage of extractive, destructive relationship with Mother Earth. With hope, we enter a stage of conscious and co-creative participation. With love, we take a step on the evolutionary ladder towards sustainable planetary communion. It is an evolutionary moment.

Honouring the Element of Water

1st WB. *(reading, then pouring water into the fountain or bowl)*

Water, an alchemy of primordial elements – hydrogen and oxygen, the spawn of stars, older than the Sun. Dancing, ever-leaping between solid, liquid, and gaseous states, the first cosmic waters inspired cosmologies, stories of creation. The primeval waters, for the Greeks, were the womb from which the god Cosmos emerged. They were the genesis of the Judeo-Christian world. Lady Science too tells an origin story. In the beginning,

86

vaporous gas rising from a young molten planet mixed with the cold winds of space to become rain.

After millions of years of rain, great tidal oceans circled the planet. In these electrically-charged, fiery, chemical cauldrons of cosmic waters was unimaginable potential, the first cell of life. In an evolutionary ritual, water speaks to this new cosmology.

E: Evolutionary Wisdom flow through me: from chaos and disorder emerges peace, order, and creation.

2nd WB. *(reading, then pouring water into the fountain or bowl)*

One drop of rain, a mighty river, a trickling brook, flowing stream, the shining lake, the aquafers and groundwaters – water is the lifeblood of the planet. Wellspring of life to each bio-region, water makes Earth the mother that suckles plant, animal, and human alike. 99% of all life exists beneath the waters. 77% water at birth, humans too are bodies of water. Water helps circulate nutrients, eliminate poisons, transport energy. We cannot exist more than four days without water. The global oceans, lungs and source of most oxygen, are larger than the atmosphere. In an evolutionary ritual, water reminds us of our deep ecology: we are one with all the Earth.

E. Evolutionary Wisdom flow through me: what we do to water we do to ourselves.

3rd WB. *(reading, then pouring water into the fountain or bowl)*

In religions and spiritualities round the world, water is the sacred element we come to at rocky places on our journey. Buddhists seek calm and serenity with water offerings. In Judaism, the Mak and Mikvah are purifying, healing baths. Christian mystic Meister

Eckhart named God the "great underground river that no one can dam up and no one can stop." Universally, water is a sign of a divine intelligence with a bias for wholeness and the power to transform suffering to joy.

In an evolutionary ritual, water speaks to an emerging spirituality: Water is sacred, not because the human declares it so, but because water is integral to all that is. Ever-changing its state of being and transforming whatever its context – rocky soil to green gardens or an embryo to a laughing child – water makes every being a vessel of new life.

E. Evolutionary Wisdom flow through me: dancing waters sing thanks to the rocks.

All chant: Come, come, comm-unity! *Drums, whistles, clapping, stomping.*

Evolutionaries' Naming Ceremony

RL. You have come believing your conscious evolution to be the number one response – ability in Earth's time of peril and promise and to name yourselves Evolutionaries. Like the banks that hold the river, we support you.

All chant: *Come, come, comm-unity! drums /clapping, stomping.*

E. *(dip branch into bowl and sprinkle water above their heads)*

Cosmic Waters that precede, are above, and around us, let Consciousness rain upon us that we might know the cosmic powers of transformation within us.

E. *(dip branch into bowl and sprinkle water above their heads,)*

Earth's Waters that flow beneath and through us, let the river of Evolution carry us beyond ways of separation and oppression to become cocreators within the whole.

E. *(dip branch into bowl and sprinkle water above their heads,)*

Sacred Waters that can destroy or create, flow through us that we might go from here to dance in the face of planetary injustice, sing of a new humanity, and become Evolutionaries for a sustainable future.

Celebration of New Evolutionary Humans

All chant: Come, come, comm-unity! *drums /clapping, stomping / recession.*

Other music: We Are One. From My Heart Is Moved album by Carolyn McDade & Friends.

Carol's bio:

Carol remembers falling in love with writing in public school. Journaling, poetry, prose, dreamwork - writing has been her life-long refuge. "It's a spiritual practice, like yoga or prayer, turning the invisible -- the mystery, fear, love, and passion -- into the visible word. It's my way of discovering and becoming myself." Perhaps it was inevitable that Carol would turn to writing to make sense of the spiritual crisis born of global warming and mass extinctions. Incorporating the emerging consciousness of interconnectivity and the new sacred story of the Universe into rituals and her own original wisdom tales, she has found a way to offer up a relevant and transforming word for these confusing and challenging times.

Carol left ministry in a Protestant Canadian Church when awakened to the urgency of the environmental crisis.

For 16 years, Carol ran the Gaia Centre for Eco-Spirituality and Sustainable Work in Algonquin Highlands, Ontario.

Carol is the author of the book 'Evolutionary Dancer.'

Water god with sacred paper made with hemp
for the purification at Katori Shrine.
(photo provided by Michiko Hayashi)

ODE TO WATER, MYSTERIOUS MAGICIAN

Fredric Lehrman (Founder of Nomad University), USA

Having no form, you are easy to recognize, as you are transparent, infinitely adaptable, conforming to every shape you find, sharing motion with whatever encounters you, lending yourself to change by your very nature. Solid when cold, evaporated when hot, you travel without passport.

Rising from deep in the earth, your gentle or ferocious touch shapes landscapes, dances with gravity, your form tailored to whatever encounters you. Generous, ready to slake the thirst of every living thing, you travel the sky with your sister, the wind, rising towards the sun as you inhale the emptiness, sometimes disguised as cloud or fog (according to the art of "weather"), then diving back down, gentle or torrential, flirting with ever-changing suitors as you return to the land.

Titanic icebergs and slow moving glaciers are your disguises, silently moving until you find your breaking point and return to the sea. But it is as ocean that you rule, where fish fly like birds through canyons beneath your surface, while whales and dolphins patrol the border above.

Intrinsically gentle, you become immensely powerful when all your molecules move in mass integration, transferring the news of earthshake or storm to foreign shores as tsunami mountains dreamed of and feared by entranced surfers. And yes, sometimes you take a vessel down with a rogue wave, reminding us that we rely on your mercy to allow us to traverse your realm.

How amazing, this water planet! The sun and the moon are beautiful, yet completely dry, as far as we know. So let us treasure the miracle of water's abundance, and remember that it surrounded and taught each of us for nine months before we left the warm womb and learned to breathe.

You flow through us every second of our lives, keeping us pliable and healthy. And isn't it convenient that the mountains just happen to function as broad reservoirs of snow stored in the high white world of Winter, ready to flow again as Spring returns, warming you, your windblown droplets descending like flocks of migrating birds revisiting lowland fields. You keep us moving, vital, alive!

This 'ode' was my way of telling l'eau how much I 'eau' her for her magic. And those remarkable French... How did they come to name those great and indispensable vehicles that crossed the uncrossable deserts, carrying enough water inside them to safely arrive at the next <u>eau</u>asis by means of their natural three-stage internal water management system, allowing Genghis Khan's armies to conquer and connect the most vast empire yet achieved by any general whose transport was dependent upon elephant, horse, or oxen alone. Only the one the French named "le cham<u>eau</u>" ...(the camel)...could do that! Oh My Eau my eau my eau my ea my eau my eau my eau...

Fredric's Bio:

 Fredric Lehrman is director of Nomad University, founded in 1974, and has lived in Seattle since 1981. His background includes professional years as a classical musician (guitar, cello, and voice), and extensive studies in psychology and spiritual traditions in many world cultures. He is the author of two books, The Sacred Landscape (1988) and Loving The Earth, a Sacred Landscape book for Children (1990), and has recorded two well-known audio courses, Prosperity Consciousness (Nightingale-Conant 1994) and Inner Factors That Control Outer Success (1998).

LOVE LETTERS TO WATER

Dr. Jason Loken (naturopathic doctor, author), CANADA

I grew up in Penticton, BC, Canada, smack between the beautiful Okanagan and Skaha lakes that bordered our small town. My two brothers, sister and I literally lived most of our summers at those beaches.

I have such fond memories of swimming, playing, water skiing and lounging at those gorgeous beaches listening to the soothing waves roll in.

I have always felt a kinship and reverence for the water, something about it just nourishes and calms my soul.

Maybe it's because of my fond childhood memories or the fact that I was born in the sign of Pisces, but I know that water carries with it not only incredible healing properties but it also helps us to connect back and remember who we truly are.

Water carries memory. I know this to be true clinically through the incorporation of using homeopathic remedies and HADO water therapy into my practice as a Naturopathic Physician and I know this personally through the time I have spent in the presence of water. Whether this be skinny dipping in a remote lake while hiking through the Rocky mountains, lounging in a natural hot spring in Costa Rica or snorkeling in the Bali Sea, something inside of me awakens through these organic experiences with water.

The awakening could be a raw feeling of exhilaration, joy, appreciation or surrender that wells up inside of me, flooding my body with beneficial neurochemistry and unlocking dormant aspects of my DNA helping me to remember the essence of who I am.

It simplifies what I have made complicated and purifies what has been distorted. Water has a magical way of bringing us back to nature and thus bringing us back to ourselves.

With great appreciation.

Jason

Jason's bio:

 With over 20 years in Natural health care and 15 years plus of post-secondary education Dr. Jason Loken ND is committed to help people reach their optimal health goals. Dr. Loken is a Naturopathic Doctor, an Osteopathic Manual Practitioner, former Registered Massage Therapist (1995-1999) and currently completing his PhD in Integrative Medicine.

Dr. Loken is former professor of the Orthopedics and Physical Medicine program at the Canadian College of Naturopathy. He lectures internationally and has appeared on both television and radio discussing topics such as mental health, disease prevention, and the fine balance in managing one's weight, hormones, and stress.

In order to best assist his patients Dr. Loken has completed additional training in the following: Walsh Mental Health Nutrient Therapy; Neurokinetic therapy; Neuro-emotional therapy; Quantum touch; Yoga physiology and therapeutics.

He is the author of two books: "Letters that Move the World; Intentional Acts of Gratitude" and "Understanding to Knowing: Unlocking Your Path to Optimal Health."

www.drJasonLoken.com

ANNIVERSARY WATER

Diana Manole (poet), CANADA

She collected rainwater in tin basins for washing the laundry and herself, but that summer there was a drought. It hadn't rained in eight weeks. She looked at the clear sky and prayed.

Then, she looked at her bulging knuckles and prayed again. She didn't know to call it arthritis but knew they hurt every time it rained. Two of her fingers were angled toward each other as if arguing. What's some pain for the joy of having plenty of water right in her courtyard?

She took off her rose-embroidered headscarf, dragged her fingers like a rake through her hair to separate the greasy strands, and sighed. Once it got that oily and heavy, it gave her headaches.

The village dirt roads were scorching and she couldn't leave barefoot. The last time she did, she had to rush back after a few steps, toes bleeding from the hardened lumps of earth. The rubber soles of her old sneakers got thinner with time, and it still felt as if walking on live coals.

Lina's well was the closest, two houses over, back in her quince orchard. She let everybody use it but if you ever stole even one fruit, you were done! No need for Lina to worry about that yet, the fruits were still small, and sour, no temptation there. It was quite difficult to turn the wheel to pull up the bucket and then pour the water over into her own bucket, but she managed. The metal cooled immediately - she fanned out her fingers on it and the joint pain subsided for a while. Such a pity she could only carry one at a time!

Right to the end, her man would throw two buckets on a yoke and go to and from Lina's smiling and singing, "Farewell, farewell, drum is beating, farewell, brave Romanians, hooray!" He had learned the march from his father who fought in the First War, who'd learned it from his own father who fought in the War of

Independence back in the 1870s. He didn't get to sing it for too long in the Second War. A grenade exploded in his hands only two weeks after he had enlisted and shattered his left arm all the way above the elbow. "Ilie Butterfly," people called him ever since, but it didn't bother him. *If 'tis true, what can you do?*

His left stump fluttered like a wing when he walked. Even he felt like laughing after he realized it! Other than that, he was strong like an ox! He worked the small piece of land behind the house, made his own wine from the grape vines he planted behind the summer kitchen, and sired seven children. True, two died young, but that was God's will, not his fault. The others were fine, all with families and children of their own but none in the same village.

Two baby storks circled around their nest on top of the recently installed electricity pole. Soon, they'd be strong enough to fly away with their parents. She always wondered where the storks went in the fall but forgot to ask Ilie. He'd been places and knew the world much better than her. She never left the village and didn't want to. Some might enjoy being looked after by their daughters-in-law like a queen mother, but that wasn't the case for her! As for her own girls... both pumped out five kids one after the other and didn't need more charges. *A load of bollocks, but they bought it*, she laughed, choked on her own saliva, and started coughing. If she still had a dark hair for each trip to Lina's well... *Phew*! Whining never makes it easier! Only the well-to-do had wells in the village and with only one hand, Ilie didn't have too many options to make money.

One more bucket and there'd be enough water for tonight. She was exhausted. *One-two-three...* she stopped every three steps, putting the bucket down and taking deep breaths before going at it again. She also cracked her knuckles and switched hands.

The sunset was near. She had to make it home before complete darkness would settle on the unlit road, but hurrying was beyond her strength. *One-two... What the hell?* She turned her head and saw Lina's tiny mutts running from the orchard toward her, growling and showing their fangs. *Damn!* Did the heat give them rabies and they broke their chains? They stopped, snarling at her, tails held high, flicking back and forth. One had white patches on its black fur coat, the other black ones on white. *Huh!* Cute like buttons and angry like sheepdogs smelling a wolf nearby.

Her instinct was to run but the bucket pinned her down like an anchor. She pitched forward, pushing it down as she fell, sharp stones and earth lumps pressing into her palms and knees. *Damn it!* She gawked at her fingers looking straighter than in a long time. The closer growling shook her out of her stupor, but she couldn't get up. She could…

Suddenly, everything became clear. She remembered the dogs' names, turned toward them, and called to them. They stopped, seemingly startled. *Yip and yap!* At the same moment, Lina showed up, a long stick in her hand, running out of the orchard. *Damn bitches! Must I keep my eyes on you all the time? Get lost or I'll skin you alive!*

The dogs left whimpering, tails between their legs, ears flat against their heads. *Lord Almighty! I ain't think anyone would come this late and I let the dogs out! I'm so sorry, auntie!* Lina kept apologizing. She helped her up, saw the scratched knees, spat on them, and swiftly rubbed them with her sleeve. *Here, dirt's off, you won't get an infection!* Then, she noticed the overturned bucket, pulled it up, and ran back to the well, cursing the dogs again.

Still mortified, Lina walked her home, carrying the water. *From now on, I'll keep 'em chained all the time! Chained like wild beasts! Lord Almighty, what could've happened*, she added, crossing herself and spitting again, this time into her bosom to scare the devil away.

She soaked herself in the tin bathtub. On Sunday evening, everybody used to take turns in the same water, first the kids, eventually Ilie and she. When their turn came, white slime coated the metal and the water was barely lukewarm, but they always enjoyed peeking at each other's nakedness with the excuse of sponging their backs. With children soundly asleep, Sunday baths often turned into belly-bumping and hee-haw. She was almost sure that they made the last one in the tub! He came out with watery blue eyes, never seen in their kin. The scrap of soap saved for special occasions smelled of roses. A Christmas gift from her oldest son!

She soaped herself and gently massaged every inch of her parchment-like skin. Her face, hands, and feet were wrinkled and greenish-brown from the sun and wind. The rest of her skin, always covered by a long buttoned up dress even in hot summers, remained fair and soft despite her age. *Like a tot's bottom*, she chuckled, tenderly rubbing her arm against her lips. Her clean hair shone as if iced with sugar.

She put on a white nightgown that she embroidered with red crosses along the v-line, hem, and cuffs, and went to bed. Ilie joined her after midnight, laughing and singing the same military march as always. His left arm had grown back, a bit longer than the left, but she kept quiet. *Why ruin the moment?*

He started asking questions about kids and grandkids, the grape vines and the small cornfield in the backyard, but he didn't answer any of hers. When he noticed the scabs on her knees, Ilie apologized for not digging a well in their backyard. *Yer know, I tried, but never got to it! First the war, then the children, and eventually...*

Before leaving, he asked for water. She rushed to pour him a glass and sprinkled wild rose petals on the surface as pink as his new set of fingernails. *Same time, same place next year?* he asked. She nodded and fell asleep happy, hoping next year it would rain in time for their wedding anniversary.

Diana's bio:

 Bucharest-born Diana Manole had immigrated in 2000 and is now proudly identifying herself as a Romanian-Canadian scholar, writer, and literary translator. In her home country, she has published nine collections of poetry and plays, earned 14 literary awards, including the National Prize for Debut in Drama from the Romanian Writers' Union and the Poetry Prize from the Association of Writers in Bucharest.

From 1996 to 2000, Diana worked as a producer/director for TV Romania International.

Among numerous cultural, sociopolitical, and human-interest shows, she is very proud of creating over 70 video poems under the title "Clipa de poezie" (A Moment of Poetry) that showcased Romanian writers.

Dr. Manole holds a Master's degree in Journalism from Carleton University and a PhD in Theatre from the University of Toronto.

She has published 14 peer-reviewed articles and/or book chapters in the US, the UK, and Canada, and co-edited a collection of essays on post-communist theatre (University of Iowa Press 2020).

She has been teaching Theatre and Performance, English and Canadian literatures, and Creative Writing at Ontario universities since 2006, including four years as an Assistant Professor in Cultural Studies at Trent.

Her seventh poetry book, *"Praying to a Landed-Immigrant God,"* is forthcoming from Grey Borders Books in Canada.

WATER

Felicia Mareels (psychic, energy practitioner), CANADA

In my growing up years most experiences with bodies of water meant we had to drive there.

The question I now ask, remembering what powerful experience happened every time we neared our destination is this; how close did we have to be before I could smell "The Lake"?

It amazes me still that I cannot differentiate what part of me would know first. Funny, until now I didn't realize that smell seemed not to be one precise sense. It was an all over experience. I will do my best to explain it with the sovereign consciousness of Innocence.

The moment I sensed the Spirit of water my heart blew open for my forever friend and I was living in the aroma of a delightful pain, an intensity that expanded my awareness of belonging in knowing more than young logic could contain.

In this overwhelm I held preciousness of infinite wisdom owning that all the distance and everything in it was mine.

My pulse would quicken and heart pounding deafness made the smell of Lake Huron intensify in a cellular urgency to be near. And from this moment until I witnessed the awesome view of her beauty - where in a fast driven moment, in a hill crested view I gasped a breath of her beautiful truth where Her blue-meets sky.

The infinite lovingness of being grabbed fierce-hold of my throat and like the first breath of birth I yelled "Yes," louder than the summer wind rushing through every open window.

"How long before we get there?"

Felicia's bio:

 For over 40 years Felicia has been a psychic intuitive/ energy practitioner, and trauma release facilitator. We are now going to hear how she discovered her calling and especially how relevant it was that she came to be named BaKa. She was raised by her mother, a psychic astrologer healer who was married to an alcoholic abuser.

Living in two worlds, Felicia learned to navigate within heightened consciousness while negotiating the trauma of a dysfunctional family.

It's possible that her intuitive attunement developed into an acute focus through empathic listening both for the desire to understand her life and her parents as well as navigating safety.

Combining Shiatsu massage and psycho/ spiritual facilitation of Transpersonal Empowerment psychology she honed an awakened intuitive focus with accuracy by developing skills and abilities of integrating these modalities into a flow and language of consciousness.

This language she discovered was discerned as a part of awareness she understood as the undeniable voice of Innocence.

For more information, you can contact Felicia at:

https://www.facebook.com/felicia.mareels1

THE MOTHER OF ALL WATER

Lars Muhl (seer, author), DENMARK

Before everything was created God's Spirit was hovering over the waters. This can be read in Genesis of The Old Testament. What kind of water is this, if nothing was yet created?

It is the water of a pregnant woman!

And the woman is the feminine Presence of God, the Spirit of Source, *Shekinah.*

Nothing or none comes into the physical world but through a woman or the feminine principle.

Water is therefore not only an element but here also a metaphor for the agent of the creative principle of life. It is the Living Water that Yeshua (Jesus) is talking about in The New Testament.

It is the same sacred water that is used in all baptismal and healing ceremonies.

Right from the beginning this water was blessed by God and is therefore the mother of ALL water!

At that moment of blessing the water was induced with healing and creative properties that can never die.

All water carries this memory of its true purpose. It must therefore always be treated with the utmost delicacy, respect and compassion. If we humans break this sacred rule we violate the very principle of life.

Through the last 200 years of industrial development we have totally forgotten the sacredness of water. We have polluted it in every way possible with all out hatred, violence, fear and disagreement. We have poisoned it by our forgetfulness of who we really are and what we were send here to do. And when we forget, the water is being robbed of its healing and creative powers.

The only thing we cannot destroy is the seed of God-consciousness, the memory of Eternity, that is always latent present in water. We only have to bless it. Bless it in anyway we can.

We can help nourishing the seed of consciousness in water by nourishing the seed of God-consciousness in ourselves, because we are also made up of 70% fluids and water.

So, by nourishing negativity we are turning the water within into poison. By nourishing love and compassion we are purifying ourselves. It is through this purification that we are able to heal the sick and resurrect the fallen.

Lars's bio:

 Lars Muhl is a Danish author, mystic, and musician, born in Aarhus, Denmark.
Already as a 10-year-old, Lars Muhl had experienced glimpses of another reality.

The shock following the sudden death of his younger sister, caused painful kundalini-like experiences, giving access to the ethereal worlds and a hypersensitive insight into other people's pain. This lasted for three years. A turning point came when Lars was 15 and received a book anonymously in the mail. Hazrat Inayat Khan's 'Gayan Vadan Nirtan' became the start of a lifelong esoteric study. Like Paulo Coelho, Lars was for many years a successful singer/songwriter who, concurrently with his music, studied the world's religions and esoteric knowledge.

Then in 1996, he was struck down by an unexplained illness, which neither doctors nor alternative therapists could diagnose.

For three years he lay in bed without being able to move or think straight. Through a close friend's intervention, Lars was put in touch with a seer who, via the telephone, brought him back to life. That was the start of a completely new existence and the beginning of that quest he has so grippingly described in his trilogy book 'The O Manuscript: The Seer, The Magdalene, The Grail'.

Along with his wife, Githa Ben-David, Lars manages the Jilale Gilalai Institute of Energy and Consciousness.

www.larsmuhl.com

River Danube separating Romania and Serbia as a liquid border

(photo taken by Claudiu Murgan)

THE WATER SPRITE

Nina Munteanu (author, limnologist), CANADA

It was a cold November day, before the snows, as I wandered the endangered Jackson Creek old-growth forest.

Centuries-old cedar, pine and hemlock towered above me, giving off the fresh scent of forest. The trees creaked and groaned, swaying in a mischievous wind. I sighed with the thought that this ancient forest might soon disappear to housing development.

Leaving the main path, I descended the leaf-strewn slope toward the river. My boots pressed through a frosty crust into the spongy ground of dead leaves and organic soil. I stopped and breathed in the fresh coolness of the air. A damp mist huddled among the trees, adding wisps of mystery to the ancient wood. It was as though I'd entered an enchanted forest in some fanciful fairy tale.

Not far from the river, I approached an old yellow birch tree. Its gnarly trunk rose as tall as some of the cedars and pines around it. Golden flakes of bark curled and formed craggy patterns around the girth of the old tree. Radiating out from the tree, moss-covered roots snaked out like tangled ropes in a profusion of brilliant green. This was fairy country, I suddenly thought.

I dropped to my knees, crouching down, and set up my tripod and camera to capture this magical tree from the perspective of the forest floor. Head almost touching the ground, I inhaled the scent of loam and decaying leaves. The fresh pungency of cedar, pine, and humid moss hung in the air.

Nearby, the river chortled and bubbled in a content symphony of motion. A curious red squirrel parked itself on a log nearby to watch me. It didn't scold me like they normally did when I entered the forest; like it understood... It then occurred to me, as I set up my equipment under the squirrel's careful stare, that I was in the presence of an enchantment. Like I was peering into a secret dance of feral celebration. But being there and appreciating it, I had now become part of it; I was Alice going down the rabbit hole into a true wonderland...

It was then that I glimpsed it as I carefully took my timed pictures. A blur of blue. What had I witnessed? A motion? A colour? Then it was gone. But in that moment, I'd felt the spark of an elation that comes with a glimpse into a secret world.

When I returned home to look at the images, I saw that my camera had captured a wispy blue entity that flowed into its view and peered around the old birch at me with a kind of curious though mischievous grin.

Had I just captured a blue sprite? *Something* was unmistakably there!

I read up on sprites. According to European lore, a sprite is a supernatural entity. They are often depicted as fairy-like creatures or as an ethereal entity. The word sprite comes from the Latin *spiritus* ("spirit"), via the French esprit. Given that the sprite I'd observed was blue and we were close to the river, I wondered if it was not a forest or wood sprite, but a water sprite.

According to alchemist Paracelsus, the term 'water sprite' is used for any elemental spirit associated with water. They can breathe water or air and sometimes can fly. They also possess the power of *hydrokinesis*, which is the ability to create and manipulate water at will. Also known as 'water nymphs' or naiads, these divine entities tend to be fixed in one place.

Sprites are not corporeal beings (like selkies, mermaids and sirens) given that they are not purely physical; they are more like local deities than animals. This explained the wispy nature of the being I'd seen peering at me from the tree.

I consulted with several friends—some who purported to know much more about sprites than I did. When friend Merridy suggested that "forest sprites, normally green, may turn blue if a nearby brook calls to them," I reconsidered, particularly when she added that "water sprites can be distinguished by their chatty nature. They rarely go beyond the banks of a river or brook. Forest sprites are mostly silent." My sprite, though quite curious, had remained silent. And yet, I felt a strong sense that it wished to tell me something.

When I told friend Craig that I would return in search of them he observed, "if you're looking for them that might be when they hide. Or maybe not. Any type of sprite is probably good, mischievous or friendly." With a spritely grin I thanked him for his advice.

I visited the forest many times after but saw no sign of any sprites. Perhaps Craig was right; they were hiding from me. But, why had I seen this shy water sprite in the first place? What was its intention with me?

There had been a kind of plaintive sadness in its rheumy eyes and timid smile. I'd felt a kindred connection somehow. More like a lost memory, buried deep in the mists of my past, shoring in my mind.

Then, on a foggy late December day, after a light snowfall, I returned to document the ice forming in the river. Islands and columns of ice had created a new topography for the flowing waters of Jackson Creek. Ice sheets also covered the forest path in places—making the walk somewhat treacherous.

At times, I had to scramble and seize hold of branches to haul my way up precipitous banks from where I'd captured sculptures of ice that formed pearls, columns and platforms on the river.

The fog grew thick as my walk eventually led me into a stand of eccentric cedars that leaned like drunks over the riverbank. The cedars sent out a tangled tapestry of gnarly roots I had to negotiate. Tingling with earth-magic energy, I dropped to my knees again and set my camera and tripod to the level of the roots.

That is when I saw the water sprite again!

This time the sprite lingered with a look of plaintive determination on its wispy hoarfrost face. It seemed to float in and out of the old cedar like the tree's own breath, inhaling and exhaling.

We stared at one another for an eternal moment before the sprite vanished in a puff of blue mist.

Again, I shared with my friends the images I'd taken of this wispy being, dressed in the blue frost of ice and snow, who'd met my stare with a timorous though determined look.

Eyes glistening like melting ice. I knew its pale face—how long I'd known that sad face of solastalgia!

In response to my photos, friend Gabriela challenged me: "did you ask what message they have for you, Nina? They keep showing up in your way, they might have a message for you or to be delivered through you to..." *whoever*... This somehow resonated with me. But how, I challenged, would I hear their message when they were silent and so fleeting? She wisely responded, "Just ask yourself the question; you might be surprised when your next thought brings the answer. Since everything is energy, and you saw them at least twice, you're probably connected with them."

I thought of what Gabriela said to me as I reviewed the photos I'd taken. It resonated. What had I thought when our eyes met for that eternal moment?

Right after my elation at being invited into this magical secret world, I thought of the forest. And the river running through it. Both are home to the sprites—their guardians. I felt a sudden dizziness at the revelation.

This century-old forest was being considered for logging to create a proposed housing development. If it went through, these ancient trees would all come down and the river would go down with it. With the forest gone, the river would also be transformed. It would be channeled underground in culverts or straightened into a lifeless gully, baking in the heat.

Without the cooling forest canopy to provide shade, the river would heat up; its life would choke. Without the rich organic loam provided by the trees, the riparian shore of the river would dry up and give up its nutrients—and its life.

All would be covered over by a merciless layer of lifeless concrete, brick and plastic.

First, the pines and cedars would come down in a thunderous maelstrom of violent screaming saws; they would crash to the ground with reverberating booms of finality. Ancient beech trees would squeal under the saws then crack with a final death shout and fall into a thunderous silence.

Then, with the clearing fires, the leaves of my precious old yellow birch would sizzle and take flight. They would join with embers of curling bark and soar in a vortex of billowing coal black fury.

All that had once clothed the earth would be destroyed, leaving only black stumps and charred debris.

The melancholy brook would flow through a killing field, itself choking with burned debris. Thick and oily, the lonely creek would grow dark and surly, smothering its own.

That was what the sprite wished to tell me: *everything is interconnected.*

If the forest goes, the water goes, the sprites go, and with them the magic of life.

I grew tearful at the thought. The sprites—the water, forest, and field sprites—had for centuries been the guardians of this enchanted wood, guarding the beauty of its service and the magic of the wild. Guarding the cycle of life.

Forced to flee their home, where would the sprites go? Condemned to seek a home in the terrifying and implacable concrete world of grey monochrome, sharp edges, and unyielding progress—where whiskered life is unwelcome— what would they do? Vilified, ridiculed, and ignored, they would lurk in the sterile domain of human hubris—doomed to shrivel into empty husks, like discarded detritus left on the side of the road along with Tim Horton's paper cups carelessly pitched from a car.

I felt dizzy with guilt. What could I do? What could one person do?...

I suddenly smile.

There is much I can do. I will start by sharing this story with you…

Nina's Bio:

Nina Munteanu is a Canadian ecologist / limnologist and internationally published author of award-winning speculative novels, short stories and non-fiction. She is co-editor of Europa SF and currently teaches writing courses at George Brown College and the University of Toronto. Her latest book is *"Water Is…"* a scientific study and personal journey as limnologist, mother, teacher and environmentalist.

"Water Is…" was recently picked by Margaret Atwood in the NY Times as 2016 'The Year in Reading'.

Her latest novel *"A Diary in the Age of Water"* will be released by *Inanna Publications* in 2020. www.NinaMunteanu.ca

THE STORY OF THE SEVEN LAKES

Claudiu Murgan (author, podcaster), CANADA

The story of the Seven Lakes surrounding the peaks of the Sacred Mountain had immemorial roots.

Word-of-mouth that had survived generations now extinct said that God had created Adam and Eve as giants, and that was the place where they had first walked as living beings.

The heaviness of their bodies had left deep recesses on the moist soil that later filled with the water with which God had blessed the land after that important creation.

Shaken by the awareness of who they were, Adam and Eve had knelt down to face each other, pushing up the ground that was now the Sacred Mountain, but only Adam's left knee had touched the ground. The other one had kept its footing, pressing hard for balance. Adam's Right Foot lake is the deepest, and some say, the most treacherous.

The mountain's dizzying heights and jagged edges were never conquered by mortal climbers on their way to fame.

Millenia had passed, and humans had learned to stay away for their own safety and gaze at the threatening peaks from a distance, getting their satisfaction by their daily fulfilment of mundane goals.

Rumors spread throughout the communities at the foot of the mountain, that the wisdom and teaching transmitted orally from gurus to yogis, were much more potent than the written ones.

Stories rolled into myths like timid spheres of snow that, when reaching their tipping point, become devastating avalanches. The few touched by the teaching neither confirmed nor denied the validity of the primordial creation or what happened after Adam and Eve were, mesmerized by the love beaming from their physical shells.

How could love and the realization they had been spirit molded into physicality, shrunk to allow for procreation and the nimble integration into what they understood was Mother?

Why had they kept to themselves the knowledge about the healing powers of their tears that, when stored in vials the size of a thimble were enough to bring health and prosperity to a whole family?

Was it true that God had imprinted the Water of the Lakes with innate intelligence and awareness as if it were a fluid-vigilante over humankind?

Historians had yet to uncover any words Adam, Eve, or of their descendants, for that matter, had written about Water's role in its time-forsaken hide-out.

Openings the size of a peephole on the sides of the six of the lakes allowed for the trickle of a whisper of the water to find its way down the slopes, hopping over stones and fallen logs, clearing layers of leaves with lost identities, resting along its arduous journey in clear puddles.

Humans and animals alike quenched their thirst from the liquid veins traversing Mother in all directions, but only a handful of them appreciated the gift of life through open prayer and thankful thoughts.

Centuries had passed before inquisitive minds acknowledged the omnipresence and omnipotence of Water. It played so many characters at once: fluid in the shape of oceans, rivers, and ponds; vapor in the invisible state of humidity and flying rivers; solid in monumental ice sculptures attached to the side of unforgivingly steep mountains and aged icecaps.

Over time, the spirituality and scientific inquiries stirred in the cauldron of evolutionary thinking, raised the unthinkable question: was Water another form of God?

Heads nodded equally in agreement and denial. Were they afraid to elevate Water to such an inconceivable level? Was it sacrilege? Water seemed to know it all, to record in its fluid molecular structure the rise and the fall of life on Earth from its inception.

Naturally, another query dropped into the pool of human consciousness: if the awakened Water seeped from the Sacred Mountain, would it contain the biological imprints of Adam and Eve?

Thoughts scattered in all directions like a beehive under a bear attack and then quieted, appalled by their intrusion into seeking the bond between God and Water. The mystery remains unsolved.

Is Water God?

Claudiu's bio:

 Claudiu Murgan is enthralled by our consciousness and the notion of our place in the enormous wheels of the multiverse. His settings as science fiction, fantasy or eco-fiction, focus on describing the beauty of Mother Nature, who demands action from all of us.

Claudiu's experience in various industries such as IT, renewable energies, real estate and finance helped him create complex, realistic characters that bring forward meaningful messages.

Claudiu is the author of three Science Fiction/Fantasy novels: The Decadence of Our Souls, Water Entanglement, and Crystal Cloud. His short stories have been published in anthologies in the USA, Canada, Italy, and Romania.

Connect at ClaudiuMurgan.com

BEFORE A SPRING

Valentine Chukwuebuka Onuorah (poet), NIGERIA

Returned I from the sojourned lashes of harmattan
Where the cracked soil of the desert hums
The anthem of every human predicament
In the furnace-prickling radiation of the sun

Coming in quantum packet of backlashes
Moments when the shrubs grow upside down
Distasteful herbs littered about the wilderness –
It's been forty-eight hours since I kissed your breast!

Is it not your fluid that lives in me
O! mountainous god of the ancient sea
From earth below and sky above, sublime
The baptism that purges my curses

I do not want to depart from your presence
Lavished royally with green and freshness
Without the blemish of man-made craftiness
But only with waterfall that reminds me the rainbow

The search for you was a search for myself
An inch closer to you gets me lost further away

And I wondered about like a rolling, rolling dice
If the two sides of this coin can become one face!

This supplication before you I say in kneels.
My amazement hung upon your legendary
That rushes speedily and wildly against time
Yet soft and slow like a newborn child

May I drink, servant and master
From your pool of purity and piety
That every blemish of the world and beyond
May by your spirit be washed away

As you unite everything living to nature
Wet and soften my heart that eyes may see
In the dry countenances of my brethren
That only you can quench our thirst.

Valentine's bio:

 Valentine Chukwuebuka Onuorah hails from Atani, Anambra State, southeastern part of Nigeria. He obtained B.Sc (Hons) in Biochemistry from Chukwuemeka Odumegwu Ojukwu University, Uli, Nigeria. He's been in love with Poetry and storytelling; and living in the center of vicious mixture of art, culture, religion and

socio-political vigorousness, his writings mirror the society of a common man, even as he focuses on the younger generation.

His latest publication: "SILENT SONGS OF A ZYGOTE: A Collection of Poems" is currently on Amazon.

As a teacher, farmer and advocate for the dignity of human lives and against hunger, he finds his voice clearer in ink, in wordings too ancient for our ancestors and too new for the now, yet unborn. While not at his desk, he surfs the net and plays soccer.

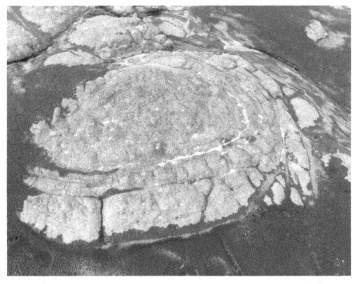

Water carvings in stone on the Coronado Beach, Panama
(photo taken by Claudiu Murgan)

SACRED WATERS

Mally Paquette (shaman), USA

To our Sacred Waters within each being and on our beloved Gaia, I overflow with gratitude for the volumes of beauty you deliver to us. I pray you find patience for our awakenings of your codes of Light! Behold and assist us with grace to discover the ceremony and wonder of the sacred.

You mirror the rainbows within us and your dazzle glimmers every aura. Blessings to the sea creatures and may we each claim ownership to live more consciously in harmony. Whales, dolphins, sharks and finned creatures we thank you for your magic and the work you do for us! Aho

Mally's Bio:

 Mally's entire life has been deeply entrenched with indigenous cultures. Her spiritual roots are embedded with Native Americans. She founded a nonprofit organization, NAAP to serve the Lakota on Pine Ridge Indian Reservation in South Dakota. For a decade she studied the Lakota traditions and in 2002, she was adopted into the Sioux tribe and cherishes this unique honour.

Mally teaches via Chakra Psychology and her intuitive gifts. She listens to the deeper bodies and can translate physical ailments offering a therapeutic new path to optimal health.

She delivers healings through traditional yoga therapy and sound vibration. The study and technique of Kundalini Tantra which Mally is immersed in can guide an individual to discover true alchemy.

SACRED STALKER

Ian Prattis (author, Zen master, shaman), CANADA

Water has always been an important element in my life. The tumultuousness of the ocean's waves and danger of hurricanes stamped a mirror for the first part of my existence, while the calmness of a winter lake reflects what the mature years look like.

Several decades ago I became aware that I had a stalker. I would glance over my shoulder. Then feel a distinct presence that persisted in following me. White Eagle Woman, my shaman mentor, made it clear I was mistaken. This was no stalker. It was a woman from the 18th century. A medicine woman from the American Southwest. She was trying to bring powerful medicine gifts to me in the 21st century. She had a name – Trailing Sky Six Feathers.

How did this come about?

When I was a young professor at Carleton University, I split my time between Ottawa, Canada, and the Hebrides in Scotland. I was trying to create an academic career and at the same time save a failing marriage. I was not doing a good job with either. I had a boat in the Hebrides, *An Dhoran* - a twenty six foot clinker built vessel, to enter the dangerous surrounding sea with tourists on board.

My teacher about the sea was Callum McAuley, Master Mariner, who held legendary knowledge of the tides, currents and landing places up and down the southern isles of the Outer Hebrides. At one time was skipper of the lighthouse tender, a boat that carried relief crews and supplies to the manned lighthouse on Barra Head, an island at the southern tip of this island chain. His position with the lighthouse tender ended when a cargo ship, the S.S. Politician, was wrecked in a storm on the small islands off Eriskay. It had a full cargo of whisky destined for the US market. Callum swiftly used the lighthouse boat to take advantage of this unexpected windfall and managed to smuggle crates of whisky ashore and hide them from the Home Guard. He was apparently very successful at this chess game, which is the reason he was relieved of his post on the lighthouse tender.

Callum became my mentor of the sea and crewman on *An Dhoran*. I listened to his fascinating stories as we pored over his charts of small boat passages, currents and tide changes. His presence on my small boat brought his vast knowledge to life. After more than forty years ashore, he was back in his natural element. It was always a struggle to keep him sober for the charter trips, but by and large he timed his drinking binges with the days when I was not putting out to sea.

One disastrous sea journey still scars my mind to this day. It was from Eriskay to the north back to my home on the Island of Barra. Before leaving Eriskay for the return journey I checked the weather forecast with a friend who lived there. A storm and fog warning was predicted for later that evening and I estimated that we would be home well before it descended. I had four tourists on board, as well as my oldest child. Iain was eleven years old at that time.

The voyage across the stretch of sea separating Eriskay from Barra was uneventful. I started to navigate down the east coast of Barra and then slammed into the unanticipated storm and dense fog. It quickly morphed into gale force winds. It was impossible to return to Eriskay. There was no place to shelter on the east coast of Barra. I knew the fierce sea conditions in the Minch, the stretch of sea that separates the islands from the mainland of Scotland, so I stayed close to the east coast of the island. The force of the storm was much more powerful than my twenty-five horsepower engine. Gale force winds swept the ocean swells to break over the prow of my boat. Sharp spray from the sea struck my face like pellets from a shotgun.

I shielded my face with one arm to better see the huge waves coming right at the boat. I maneuvered *An Dhoran* so she was at an angle to the waves and could crest over the swells and not be battered to pieces from the storm.

My teenage son, Iain, used the boat hook to fend off the following dinghy from smashing into the stern of the boat. I felt myself entering a terrible, cold silence while braced at the wheel. There was no mind there, only an intuitive awareness of danger in this moment, then danger in the next moment. Navigation was just far enough away from the inshore spurs of rock jutting out like razors. The no-mind mariner at the wheel stood quietly muttering the 23rd Psalm, "I shall not want." I turned *An Dhoran* through a narrow gap in an offshore rock spur. I caught a swell as it crested through the gap, spinning the wheel hard to port to avoid the ragged edge of another rock ledge. Then quickly to starboard to find a more sheltered stretch of sea. I did not have that knowledge. I did not have that skill. It was beyond my capabilities. This was not learned from Master Mariner Callum McCauly. My mind simply did not operate, yet I had a seamless connection to a furious sea. A powerful instinctive knowledge took over as I felt an ethereal female presence guiding me through.

My friends on Eriskay, on seeing the worsening weather had quickly telephoned the houses and crofts on the east coast of Barra to turn on every light. Iain remembered their urgent message: *"Prattis left Eriskay an hour ago and is across the sound. He cannot turn back in this storm. Needs all your lights switched on to help him navigate."*

I noticed houses bordering the coastline with every light on – and that gave me navigation marks to get back to Castlebay. The frightened tourists sat inside the cabin for weight at the front end of the boat as the sea smashed into the creaking clinker boards. This extra ballast saved the timbers of our vessel from being split open. Something else had their hands on the wheel. The slow progress down the coastline of Barra continued under a mantle of desperate prayers. Later we limped slowly into the sheltered harbour of Castlebay. The mother of my children and then wife was there to gather Iain and take him home. The phone call that we were rounding the tip of Barra brought her to the dock at Castlebay harbour with blankets for my son and a fierce glare at me. We were not on good terms. The passengers disembarked with great relief.

I moored *An Dhoran* at her berth in the bay next to the Castle. The wind was dropping and the fog began to clear. Callum and I rowed to shore in the dinghy, then with ropes pulled it back to its mooring place. It sat there gently bobbing across from the Post Office and the small boat pier. Callum had been totally silent throughout the journey from Eriskay, which was most unlike him. He had been watching me. And praying. Callum McAuley, Master Mariner, said to me in a shaky voice, "Ian boy, I don't know how the hell you did that. In all my years I have never seen anything like it."

"Callum, I don't know about that either," I replied in a hoarse, bewildered whisper.   "THAT" became even more penetrating, as next day the news reported that the storm had taken down a sixty-foot trawler in the middle of The Minch. It had spared my small boat.

With the money from the passengers in my pocket, I beckoned to Callum to come with me.

"Callum, you're coming with me to the Castlebay Bar."

Callum shook his head and reminded me that he had been banned from the bar for twenty years now.

"Not tonight," I grimly said.

I remember that he looked at me with a touch of both fear and amazement. We walked up the hill to the Castlebay Bar. Callum was reluctant to step inside and as soon as he did, Roddy the bartender came over to throw him out.

"Roddy, he's with me tonight," I said. There was something steely in my voice that immediately caught Roddy's attention. He paused for a moment as he had already heard about our journey from Eriskay. News travels fast on the island. He looked from Callum to me and then reluctantly nodded his consent. Callum was quickly surrounded by some of his seafaring friends eager to hear him tell the story. I greeted his cronies, who were delighted in this rare occasion. I placed two ten pound notes on the counter, the sum total of my earnings from a day of insanity on the sea.

"Roddy, this will cover me tonight."

Roddy filled a glass tumbler with his best whisky. "We'll not be taking your money my friend. Everyone is relieved you are back safely from Eriskay."

A long row of full whisky glasses appeared on the wooden bar I was wearily leaning against. Callum told and retold the story of the day's journey on *An Dhoran,* over and over again, each time more elaborate than the previous. I did not listen. My hands shook as I took the glass of whisky from Roddy's huge fist. My mind was frozen. The cold silence told me it was not I who brought the boat home safely.

At closing time, I thanked Roddy for allowing Callum his night of storytelling and walked over to the table where he was taking our voyage into mythological realms. Callum still had a full glass of whisky in front of him.

"Time to go Callum, maybe you don't need that final shot."

"Indeed I do," he replied with as much dignity as he could muster: "I could be dead tomorrow, so there's no point in leaving it sitting here, is there now."

He downed it and I helped him out of his chair and walked him home to the small cottage in Leidag he shared with his sister Morag. He was singing and fell over a few times, stopping to tell me the story of the voyage as though I did not know the details of it. I eventually delivered him to his cottage and coaxed him into his comfortable armchair. He promptly fell asleep. I walked to my home, overlooking the bay. I could see the Castle and the islands to the south shrouded by the soft light from the quarter moon. It was calm and peaceful, nothing like the earlier hours on the sea. Sitting on the steps of my house, I went over in my mind this dangerous day. My reflections were savage, yielding ugly truths long buried.

I thought of the line of whiskies at the bar, a celebration of returning from the furious sea. There was nothing to celebrate. A rebuke was needed for my recklessness in endangering the lives of others, including my first born son. I could take no credit for bringing *An Dhoran* home. I thought of the tumultuous sea as a piercing dirty grey, the color of dying – just waiting for me. I knew that I was not in the right place internally and did not belong here. I had obscured this true confession with blind recklessness. The shrouds fell away and I could see just what I'd allowed myself to become.

I was no heroic captain at the wheel, just stupid, reckless and displaced. I had to put an end to my madness on the sea. This was not my domain in life. This beautiful island in the Hebrides was not where I was to be. The stressful drain on time and energy travelling back and forth between Canada and the Isle of Barra was debilitating. It left me with zero life-force energy for the work I was destined to touch. I was merely surviving amidst the suffering of being totally misplaced. So down I went into the graceless oblivion that alcohol and depression permits.

I stood up slowly and stepped into my house. Still in the grip of that awful, chilling silence, I stretched out on the large sofa in the kitchen. My border collie Bruce crept over and rested his chin on my chest to provide comfort. I knew I had to change the course of my life and emerge from the swamp I had created. This deadly sea voyage was the signal to embark on a deep internal spiritual journey. They were not my hands on the wheel.

On my return to Canada after this brutal summer, I met White Eagle Woman at an elders gathering. Her air of quiet authority immediately struck me. She looked into me deeply and saw that I needed help. She had been instructed by her ancestors to train me and it began straight away with an eight day vision quest, prelude to a thirty year period of training and healing under her guidance. This allowed the mosaic of the past to reveal itself. She identified Trailing Sky Six Feathers for me and revealed the guardian role held by her. White Eagle Woman also taught me how to create a medicine wheel in my mind. I was always to start by bringing into my mind the ancient shaman from the East, then the South, West and North in succession, finally to bring in the ancient shaman from the Centre. She told me to see this as a map in my mind. I was instructed to call forth the animal guides I had personally experienced, again starting from the East. I had experienced many animal guides and told her so.

White Eagle Woman retorted with some exasperation:

"Choose the most powerful ones, dammit!"

With that cryptic encouragement, I chose mountain lion in the East, moose in the South, deer in the West and medicine bear in the North, with dolphin and whale below and the great eagles above. The space at the centre of the mental medicine wheel was the sacred still-point, a conduit for me to dialog with Trailing Sky Six Feathers – but only when connection to the sacred mystery was intact.

When I died in her arms in 1777 she vowed to find me in the future. She refused to give up on how dense I was in present time. Through her insistent guidance, my karma was reversed. The internal battles ceased. I learned to navigate past and present life experiences over four centuries. The medicine gifts required that I nurture skills to use them wisely. A clear mosaic of experiences stretching back to 1777 was in my mind.

Once the Vision Quest with White Eagle Woman was complete, I carefully built the medicine wheel in my mind and spoke to Trailing Sky about the sea journey.

"Trailing Sky, was it you that brought my boat safely home?" I already knew the answer.

"You were there on all the other dangerous voyages – were you not Trailing Sky?" I said softly to her, affirming her guardian presence.

She responded after a long pause.

"I had to keep you alive, your son too, for he receives the Torch after your passing. I kept you alive when you almost lost your right arm in a foolish fight in Vancouver. I also kept you alive when you were dying in India."

Flashing through my mind were all the moments when death had faced me in this lifetime. She had always been there whenever my life was at risk and brought me through to safety. I took our dialog to another level,

"When I die, will you be there? What will happen to you?"

Her voice was soft and precise. "When you die, I will be the last portion of your consciousness to dissolve. Before that moment of dissolution I will guide both of us as one integrated mind into the next adventure." I was stunned into a long silence and refrained from asking about the next adventure. Trailing Sky Six Feathers is not an illusion, a projection I am attached to. She constitutes all that is crystal clear and wise within me - the ultimate Muse. I stayed very quiet until it was late in the night. I knew she was listening in to my thoughts. Just before midnight she quietly said to me,

"You have transformed all that you brought in with you and suffered from in this life. The person who stumbled blindly through the first part of your life is not the Ian walking through the second part of life. In India, Arizona, France, the Canadian wilderness and around the world you went to extraordinary lengths to deal with karma. You changed course and now have freedom and alignment. There were so many severe experiences, but you responded by moving in a spiritual direction. You touched universal threads that allowed me to keep my promise from 1777. And we are both grateful for that."

125

I could feel her smile expand along with my own. I placed my two hands together with great reverence and offered a deep bow of gratitude to Trailing Sky Six Feathers.

Namaste.

Ian's Bio:

Dr. Ian Prattis is Professor Emeritus at Carleton University in Ottawa, Canada. He is an award-winning author of eighteen books. He received the 2011 Ottawa Earth Day Environment Award and in 2018 the Yellow Lotus award from the Vesak Project for spiritual guidance and teaching dharma. He is a Poet, Global Traveler, Founder of Friends for Peace, Guru in India, Zen teacher and Spiritual Warrior for planetary care, peace and social justice.

He studied Tibetan Buddhism in the early 1980's, Christian meditation with the Benedictines, and was trained by Native American medicine people and shamans in their healing practices.

He also studied the Vedic tradition of *Siddha Samadhi Yoga,* and taught this tradition of mediation in India (1996 – 1997).

He has travelled widely on this beautiful planet and gives talks and retreats in Canada, India, Europe, the USA and South America.

The basic commitment he holds is to make the world a beautiful place by encouraging people to embrace their true nature. His teaching focuses on the spiritual issues of the day and honours all traditions.

www.IanPrattis.com

WATER IS LIFE IS LOVE IS WATER

Kayden Radhe (entrepreneur), NEW ZEALAND

Water is Life
Life is Love
Love is Water is Life is Love

Water is Holy
Every Drop is sacred
Water is Divine
Nectar of Creation

Thank you Ocean
Lakes Rivers Streams
Cleansing Rains
Living Springs

Water is Listening
Truthfully Revealing Water is Conscious
Vibrational Healing.
Water is Life
Life is Love
Love is Water is Life is Love

Kayden's bio:

Meet the Founder of Blue Bottle Love, Kayden Radhe. She is a woman dedicated to sharing the eco-friendly beauty and high vibration frequency of these blue glass water bottles which serve to enhance and heal the consciousness of water. She lives in Maui, Hawaii in her Blue Bottle Love Temple Home. She is totally IN LOVE with bringing Blue Bottle Love to the world! This has become a fully encompassing passion, and the love keeps growing! The energy behind these bottles...as well as the beauty of these bottles has captured practically all of her attention, and she absolutely loves to focus on these babies — leading to some pretty magical photos in the Blue Bottle Love world.

A peaceful view of Simcoe Lake along the
shores of Town of Innisfil, Ontario, Canada
(photo taken by Claudiu Murgan)

LET WATER LIVE

Geraldine Sinyuy (poet), CAMEROON

Water is life

Water is love

Water for life,

Water for the seeds to grow

Water for the fishes in the seas,

Water for transportation

Water for cleansing

Water for restoration.

No water, no life.

No water, no food,

No water, no sea transport

No water, no trees

No water, no fish,

No water, no beauty.

Save the water, save lives.

Pollute the water, you pollute life.

No water no firmament,

The water existed before mankind,

Honour water, respect water.

No water, no castles high and huge

No water, no chemistry and apothecary,

No water, no beer, no wine, no juice.

Water is needed by both great and small,

It's the most basic need of mankind, fauna and flora.

No water, no Timbuktu,

No water, no trees, no voyages by ship,

Life would be impossible without water,

And all would be deserts,

Human beings baked

Like sand in the desert,

And all entrails crushed

and crumbled under touch

like soaked chalk.

Without water all would be wild storms of dust

Unleashed from the bowels of an enraged nature!

Wind and sun go rampage

Thus drought in the land!

Hungry starveling and thirsty souls

Skeletal dehydrated ghosts

Gape in the heavens

Eyes sunk deep in dryness,

Lips unable to pray

Clipped together for lack of saliva!

Fish and hippos forever united
To sand and mud
No surgical separation possible!
This will be the fate of man without water?
Let water live!

Before

Before you waste a glass of water,
Think about a weary traveler in the desert.
Who longs to have just a drop on his lip.
Before you waste a bucket of water,
Think about those who travel a thousand miles
And dig a million metres
Just to get a cup of water.
Before you waste hours in a shower,
Think about those who haven't bathed for months.
Before you pollute water,
Think about those who depend on it,
The people, the fish
And life aquatic
Before you toss away that bucket of used water,
Think about recycling.
Before you let the rain water waste,
Think about the drought.

Geraldine's bio:

Cameroonian born Sinyuy Geraldine trained as an English Language and Literature Teacher at the University of Yaoundé in Cameroon where she obtained a Secondary and High School Teacher's Diploma in 2005. Geraldine earned her PhD in Commonwealth Literature from the University of Yaoundé in 2018 and currently teaches English Language and Literature at Government Bilingual High School, Down Town Bamenda.

She is a book review/contributing editor at *WordCity Monthly Journal;* co-editor/contributing author of the poetry anthology, *Poetry in Times of Conflict*; and author of *Music in the Wood: and Other Folktales*.

Sinyuy passionately advocates for organic gardening and environmental care.

She has had the following awards; Featured Change Maker at World Pulse #She Transforms Tech Featured Change Makers Program.

Featured Storyteller on World Pulse Story Awards, May 2017.

Prize of Excellence as Best Teacher of the Year in CETIC Bangoulap, Bangangte, 23 October, 2010.

She is also Winner of the British Council Essay Writing Competition, Yaoundé, 2007, and Winner of Short Story Runner-Up Prize, *Literary Workshop*: CRTV Bamenda, 1998.

WIND AND RAIN

David Solomon (author, mentor, thought leader), USA

"Our mind creates the world, but before that, the world creates our mind.

Until we see that, we are doomed to live in that world."

-Buddha

Weather control is known throughout all indigenous cultures.

Whether by dance, rune or word, affecting the natural forces around us is an ability long since used at times of need.

We can affect the world around us through directly physical means. This is one of the easiest types of Manifestation, as the subtle forces that give rise to wind are some of the easiest to measure, via a technique known as Aerokinesis.

I first learned Aerokinesis in Damanhur, a mystery school in the tradition of Atlantis, in Italy. Before I explain what occurred, a comment on the relationship between intention and action: I remember having dinner with a friend, Allen, and casually pointing two fingers at a small jar on the table. My hand was resting next to my plate, and the fingers were pointing subtly. I was sending energy, hoping the jar would move. My attention was on it mentally, but my eyes were on him, physically.

Amidst discussion of politics, business and culture, Allen suddenly picked up the jar and moved it nine inches to the left. He didn't use it for anything, just shifted its position on the table. Was that telekinesis, or nonverbal signaling? Was it less "special" because the jar was picked up by human hands, and didn't slide on its own? For everyday things, direct physical action on the material plane is easier (for most of us) than action through the Ether / Astral, or through the higher Causal planes.

Since higher dimensions that enclose lower dimensions like the third, astral and causal influences affect everything that occurs in the third dimension of space-time. Without the jar teleporting or rays of electricity shifting it, my intention, one way or another, manifested.

While me picking up the jar and moving it may have been easier physically, this effect does not always scale. Moving a building, for example, originates in will just as moving a jar or rock does. Yet as a solitary influencer, you would be well served working on higher causal planes, and seeing your intentions carry through the astral vibration into the wills of mortals who use their third dimensional bodies to carry out the task.

Keep that in mind as you consider the stories of any Magician. Mechanism of action should never be confused with the effectiveness of a Magical act; it's far easier for the universe to manifest miracles through seemingly normal means than to produce a sparkly purple flying turtle that grants your every wish (though I'm working on this one...).

If you're with someone and their leg is bleeding, and you have the option of only sending intention or holding intention while applying a bandage. Sometimes, the solution is right there in front of you - and denying it in the games of Specialness and Attachment can often cause more harm than good. Magic is here when we need it, and though infinite, should not be wasted, or taken for granted.

* *

Joseph Filch, an ordinary man with deep faith, was walking home one day when he heard the town's flood sirens go off. The hurricane off the coast was drawing nearer, and just as the sounds hit his ears, the rain started to fall.

After several hours of increased winds and rising water levels that turned the street into a series of rivers, then a growing pond, Joseph watched, silently, and prayed to be saved...

First his porch is soaked, then the entire first floor, so he climbed upstairs and watched through a bedroom window.

He prayed again, and Elizabeth Andrews, his neighbor, floats by on a raft. "It's looking pretty bad, Joseph! Want a ride?"

"No thanks," he says. "God will save me!"

She paddles on with an exasperated look on her face, and mutters something to the two beings who did join her - two shivering white poodles - wrapped in blankets.

The waters keep rising, and he's forced onto the roof. After more prayers, a helicopter arrives, hovering overhead. He waved them off, confident in his miracle. Shaking their heads, the pilots leave to save another soul.

Eventually, abandoned by the people of the city, deluged by heavy rains and water levels above all nearby buildings, Joseph drowned.

At the Gates of Heaven, he shook a strength finger at God. "Why didn't you send help? I prayed and asked for a miracle! It was the most important one of my life!"

God looked at him, raising an eyebrow. She said, "I sent you a warning, a boat, and a helicopter. What more did you want?"

* *

Joseph's mistake is that he didn't ask for something specific and didn't recognize a miracle when it happened. Had he asked for the waters to recede...well, that's something I've only heard of Amma achieving.

As for one of my own weather miracles, I'm not yet a world traveling spiritual teacher, so I went for something smaller. More realistic, more acceptable as possible to my rational mind - which if you remember, is a key and essential ally in any and all Magic.

* *

I was having dinner with friends at a tasty Ethiopian restaurant near Stanford. The talk was lighthearted and casual, about our lives, our jobs, and the silly funny things that arise after a glass of wine. It was fun, but after an hour I started to feel not quite at home.

I asked everyone why ducks don't fly upside down (because then they'd quack up!) and used the groans as a cue to step outside for a breather. It was 2016, and I was deep in shamanic training.

I could feel the energy, emotions and to some extent, thoughts of everyone in the crowded restaurant, and it was all a bit too overwhelming. Breathing deeply of night air, I noticed, in addition to the crispness of fall cold, that the air was moist. It smelled like rain.

Closing my eyes, I extended my consciousness up and out. I could feel the electric tingles of a storm brewing, and noticed that the leaves on nearby trees were cupped, that none of the customary squirrels or birds seemed to be around.

My car was parked a few blocks away, and the windows were open. Rather than go to it, close them, and head back, I took this as a sign. My intuition to return to peaceful solitude was drowned out by this nagging "should" ego-voice demanding I be more social, reminding me of my marathon of cave-like seclusion of long meditations and journeys away from other people.

The cognitive dissonance of a soul not fully embodied... Yet I was aligned enough with my inner knowing of the perfect and best path to follow. I also wanted to stay disciplined, to stick to my schedule, and stay productive - take that, O Egos of Desire. I sometimes regret leaving the fun, exuberant mood - outings like that were rare. But the part of me that wanted to leave was victorious.

My friend Xing seemed to be getting antsy, and with a few whispers, we agreed that we both wanted to head back.

136

A few more duck jokes and words about some new startup, and we left. And in the ten minutes since I first stepped outside, the moisture had turned into a drizzle.

Walking in our California T-shirts was no longer an option, so we ran to my car as fast as we could, the raindrops increasing to a downpour literally with every step.

"What the heck?!" Xing said - for as soon as we got in the car, the rain was so heavy that we could barely see past the windshield! We apparently left at the perfect time.

I drove, slowly with the lights and wipers on, with the cautious drivers in what was one of the heaviest rains of that year. This was just before the California Drought (which a Wikileaks obsessed friend named Devin later told me was manmade), so the rain was weird, but not extraordinary.

We made small talk, and finally arrived at home. As we were pulling up into the driveway, I said, "Hey, Xing, wanna try a spiritual experiment?"

"Um...maaayyybe. Will it take a long time? I need to finish an essay."

"Nope! Let's cap it at 5 minutes. We can stay here in the car, and...wanna make it stop raining?

That way when we leave to go inside, we won't get soaked! Plus, it would be pretty cool."

(Clearly my levels of reverence for Magic were below average...as is completely okay for abilities that are our human rights to claim! Though reverence is better, especially if you want divine support, but I digress...)

"Okay, sure." She said. "What should we do?"

Xing agreeing right away was almost miracle enough! I rarely co-created miracles with anyone back then, and having someone believe in you - especially for something as uncommon as Magic in the technology obsessed hub of Silicon Valley. Even though we were friends and I felt comfortable with Xing - and even though she was exploring spirituality in her own way - this was a welcome surprise.

"Cool."

A pause, brief...then, I allowed the knowing to flow forth. Everything we were about to do, everything that would happen, flashed through my clairvoyant sight in seconds.

"Let's start by holding hands" I said, more authoritatively while remaining lighthearted.

"Let's close our eyes and breathe deeply."

Speaking slowly, I led us through a relaxed exercise to quickly induce trance. We breathed slowly and deeply into our bellies, and let our mouths open, our faces relaxed. Where we let go of every thought, worry and care. Where we relaxed completely into the present moment. All was well.

A visualization came next, words to expand our awareness as a knowing of ourselves as beings in a car, and at the same time, beings of cloud, surrounding the area. We were in these bodies, and we were part of the thick, the wide, the expansive.

Wetness, rich condensation was also part of our awareness, as connected and intimate as our very skin. We were humans, and we were clouds. We had legs, chests and hands - and we were also this collective, united with the wind, feeling action and reaction as one.

We were all that we saw and felt, inner and outer, linked together as one awareness in the universal Body of God.

And we receded. We that were the clouds pulled ourselves back from a space above the we that were also the bodies, and we retreated into a space farther away.

The rain, which had been pounding at the windshield up until that point, lessened. The scattering *drip-drip-drip-drip-drip* decreased

138

over a very short time, in that level of consciousness where time held meaning, and yet it did not. When the rain had ceased by about 70%, Xing opened her eyes and said "Woaaaaah."

Downpour! Suddenly all the relaxation of the storm reversed and the windshield was again drenched, the drip-drip-drip-drip-drip back to what it was in the beginning.

"No!" I said. "We can't act surprised! This isn't wishful thinking. It's like raising our arm. It just…it just is. Let's try again...and hold the intention. Let's be peaceful, still, calm, until the rain is totally gone. We need to hold it. And then we can't be in disbelief. We need to be in gratitude and awe, in appreciation and respect."

Xing breathed. "Okay, okay. Sheesh. You take this really seriously David. Alright, let's do it again."

Again the hands. This time, without the words. Internally, we repeated what we had done before, and the rain became less, less, less...

There were still a few drips, but we were also under a tree, who's leaves could have been soaked.

I opened the car door, slowly. Nothing fell inside. I put a hand out. One or two drops from the tree. I got out of the car, stood up. Looked around. No rain anywhere near us.

Xing did the same. Farther down the street - over the row of trees that bordered us and the main road - we could see rain falling in the distance, about 150 feet away.

In the opposite direction, past the house and just past the neighbor's yard, we saw the blur of rain still falling.

Awe. Gratitude. Stillness. The creeping smile of victory, forming on my face. It was going all the way up to my eyes.

Magic was Real, and it was awesome.

I turned the car back on. The clock read 10:56, exactly 6 minutes from when we started.

"We did it," I said. "We did it in 5 minutes. The last minute was us standing outside the car, appreciating everything."

Xing didn't argue. We felt so peaceful, so surreal. Analyzing that statement or talking about anything else didn't seem to matter.

As we went inside, one of my ego's wonderful sub-personalities (we all have between 8-80 according to Damanhurian Spiritual Physics) - the personality that gets really excited and ambitious, said "Hey Xing, is it OK with you if I share this story and mention you by name? Will you back me up? This kind of thing could really change the world!"

"Um...sure. Who are you going to tell it to?"

"Just close friends for now. If I say something more widely, I can change your name. Unless you're up for doing a video..."

"Naaaah. Close friends are fine though. That was really cool."

"That *was* really insanely friggin awesome. Wanna make the rain come back?"

"Let's not jinx it."

We laughed. A true co-creator she was, able to follow and lead as the energies shift.

I vowed to myself to reverse the process and summon rain at a later date. About a year later, I succeeded twice, once after another dinner with three friends in a quiet, woodsy backyard in Los Altos.

My friend Rosalio brought a magnificent, gemstone-covered, copper-wrapped wand, and we all used it to share a prayer or wish. During that time - when the drought was in full swing - I wanted these abilities to become more active.

During my turn, after a long, trance induced invocation, a BOOM of thunder shook the heavens, the leaves...and in a few minutes, we all had to pack up and move inside.

Back to Xing. After enjoying the awe of our little Miracle, we went in the house. Two friends were in the living room, one studying, the other working on a Macbook.

"Hey guys, we just stopped the rain in a big sphere around the house! Xing was with me, we did it together! Right, Xing?"

She looked at me, then at their skeptical expressions. Cringing a little, slightly hesitant, she said, "Ummmmm, surrre...yeah...I mean, it could have stopped on its own, but it was fun trying."

What?!

Ah, progress made, progress lost. Just another exercise in detachment.

Seriously though, I was miffed...until I realized that seeing Real Magic live can dramatically influence one's karma, and the higher forces, which are always helping our spiritual growth can sometimes affect our memories in certain ways.

I lost touch with Xing after she moved out but saw her from time to time, and she ended up working with a friend who was deep in the middle of his own spiritual journey.

Perhaps before this incarnation started, she, as a genderless, infinitely-named soul decided on a certain path in life, and unlike mine, Magic wasn't to be a focal point for her - or at least not yet.

As part of a process of Awakening to your true divine nature, seeing or performing Magic is sort of like being given the powerful tools of a surgeon, general or parent. You may be able to wield them, but if you aren't prepared, aren't ready, sometimes delaying - or even saying no - to those things may be what's in your highest good.

Magic isn't for everyone, and while it's thrilling if it is for you, it is also just one path of spiritual growth.

For you to honour your path as a Magician (or not, if you're realizing thus) is honouring your authentic truth to yourself.

You'll find your community, or build one, which is what I've been doing since this whole thing started.

As wind, as rain, as man and ice and snow: I wish you a good day.

David's bio:

 David Solomon's purpose is to discover, improve and teach Real Magic by building the best mystery school in the world. He is a Channel and a Magician with training in multiple traditions by masterful human, divine, and extraterrestrial teachers and lineages, including the Atlantean school of Damanhur. His experience of over 222 miracles, synchronicities and Siddhis of rapid healing, manifestation, materialization, weather control, telekinesis and other phenomena led him to write "Magic is Real: How to Create Reality, Manifest Miracles and Make Spirituality Fun Again!"

The system of Open Sourced Magic he uses is intended to support divine embodiment and the building of temples of Thoth, Lakshmi and Aphrodite, as well as launching the future city Atlantis Reborn in 2041.

David teaches workshops on third eye opening, astral travel, channeling, Causal-plane 5D Soul Healing and manifestation, past life integration, and life purpose alignment.

To request a workshop, talk, private session, or join an upcoming Magical Mastermind, please visit MagicalGoldenAge.com.

WE SHALL RETURN

Anaiya Sophia (author, mystic, storyteller), FRANCE

I live in the Cathar region of the French Pyrenees, an area associated with the Celt's, Mary Magdalene, and then later, the Cathars. The countryside is primarily rural farming land with a scattering of quaint French villages. But, from there, the terrain starts to close in as the mountains begin to rise from the valley floor, flanking the road beside the crystal clear rivers.

The colours change from verdant greenery soaking in the summer sun to vibrant shimmering golds as the air begins to noticeably cool.

The buildings also vary, from rustic, bohemian cottages to steep-raked roofs that can cope with the promise of winter snows and horizontal blizzards.

I have always felt the enormity of this place and often catch a glimpse of what happened in these mountains hundreds of years ago. And how those memories are as potent and rich today.

No one can deny the power and presence that dwells here. Despite the Pyrenees being a relatively young mountain belt, many of the rock formations are much older than the Alps.

For thousands of years, many tribes and traditions have made their way to the Pyrenees seeking spiritual sustenance and evolution. The telluric energy that flows through these peaks and valleys creates a bridge between our world and another.

Les Contes, the name of our house, is the last property as you climb your way through the towering gorge toward the village and chateau of Montsegur, known as the last Cathar stronghold.

143

Situated at the confluence of two rivers and beside a holy spring, those who feel a strong resonance with the feminine, especially Mary Magdalene, will discover a place strongly rooted in her tradition.

There is a spring at the back of the house called La Source de Belisama, whose waters bubble up from Mt. Soulerac, the Cathar holy mountain that towers above Montsegur. The faithful say this is where Esclarmonde the Great now lives, guarding the mysteries and location of the grail.

Belisama is the Celtic goddess of rivers and springs, whose name always reminds me of the Italian word for beautiful - 'bellissima'. Belisama was a Gaulish goddess whose name meant "the brightest one" or "the most powerful."

Her presence is still honoured today, with many local towns and villages named after her. Some locals claim to be descendants of this most loved goddess, calling themselves 'the sons and daughters of Belisama - the shining ones.' And I must say, since drinking these waters I have indeed started to glow.

I understand there have been many experiments regarding this water and its pathway down through the gorge into the valley.

For centuries people used to say it just disappeared. This once gushing river, central to local Cathar pathways, seemed to just dry up, as gallons of water just evaporated.

However, in the '90s, experiments were underway to follow the water and see where in fact it did go. By placing natural dye in the water at the higher peaks, the results revealed how the mountain stream entered an unseen cave that led into the 'pog' of Montsegur.

Now the stream was turning into an underground river that wound its way through the vaults and crevices of the last Cathar stronghold, and once Solkar Temple, before resurfacing at the back of our house, in four small springs and one mighty one - La Source De Belisama.

These mountains and their waters have been sacred for as long as anyone can remember, perhaps for thousands of years before Christianity.

Most of the landmarks that are now sacred to Our Lady and her teachings were places of ancient power. Usually, they possessed holy springs, and are found at the confluence of two rivers.

They were major centres of learning, built into the mountains by God. That is why there are so many legends of Mary Magdalene in grottoes beside a spring.

She and others before her utilized the natural shelters and waters that existed throughout the South of France as her meeting places to begin her teachings. They were convenient, required no construction, and were well hidden.

Since the people already respected these places as holy sites, they went to hear her knowing that the wisdom she brought was also sacred.

In 1321 the last Cathar Parfait, Guilhem Bélibaste, when being burnt at the stake, uttered a prophecy for all to hear, "In 700 years we shall return again".... well, of course, that time is now.

And so, when I gaze upon and drink these sacred waters, I indeed sense and praise the goddess Belisama, but I also see the resurgence of the Faith and Wisdom of Mary Magdalene. I see Guilhem's prophecy gushing to the surface for the people to drink from.

For seven centuries, this water has been hidden within the earth, quietly biding its time in the vaults and caverns of Montsegur, the ancient grail castle.

It is surfacing again now, enlivened by a spirit whose time is now. And the many, many things that were once tragically forsaken— need to wait no more, as what was once lost things become found again.

Anaiya's bio

 Anaiya Sophia is a Mystic, Storyteller, Soul Oracle and Author of Revelatory Wisdom. She teaches workshops throughout the world and is best known for the creation of *Sacred Body Awakening*. Known for showing up as a trailblazing resource of unapologetic truth and transparent courage, her heart is both fierce and tender.

She carries an oral message that stirs the remembrance of a continuous lineage with the Feminine Principle that throughout the centuries has preserved its spiritual dignity, without the need for permission or recognition from any other source.

Several of her books are:

The Grail King, Part III: Logo's Story (Lulu, 2020)

Fierce Feminine Rising (Inner Traditions, 2020)

Sacred Relationships (Inner Traditions, 2015)

The Rose Knight, Part I: Sophia's Story (Lulu, 2014)

Anaiya lives in the Cathar region of Southern France with her beloved husband Pete Wilson. Together they run a B & B at the base of Montsegur where individuals, families and large groups can come and stay.

Anaiya is able to conduct Baptism, Marriage, Divorce and Death Ceremonies as there is a Chapel and Spring on site. www.anaiyasophia.com

SAROVAR SACRED LAKE – Golden Temple
India (*From my visit to the holy Lake, India*)

D. G. Torrens (author), UK

The lure of the Sarovar Lake in the heart of the Golden Temple, India, was a journey I was destined to make.

I had heard a great deal about the spiritual and mystical stories connected to the historical and sacred water. I was neither a sceptic nor a believer, simply put, an open-minded mother who worried about her young eczema and asthmatic suffering child since her birth.

My husband, five-year-old daughter, and I were travelling from the United Kingdom and we were visiting a family in Delhi. Before our journey began, I insisted that we visit the Golden Temple while in India.

I had learned of the sacred lake's healing powers and wanted to experience the ritual of walking into the lake with my daughter. We had tried every cream suggested, prescribed, and researched for my daughter's skin, and that to no avail. Some medication reduced the severity of her condition, but only marginally. By this time, I was applying her skin cream during the summer months up to twelve times a day to prevent her skin from drying out. It was heart-breaking to see my daughter suffering. I was ready to try anything. Faith and confidence in the unknown were a step that I felt compelled to follow.

But before I continue with my incredible experience, I will share with you a fascinating story/legend, surrounding Sarovar Lake that dates back hundreds of years. It is a story that is synonymous with the Golden Temple, a sacred place of pilgrimage for many, and most importantly, a motif to experience a spiritual healing for my daughter and myself.

A sacred tree called the *Beri Tree* is an old jujube tree, which stands on the eastern side of the Golden Temple, said to contain mysterious healing powers. The *Beri Tree* with its mythical history is close to Sarovar Lake within the temple grounds where it has grown for centuries.

According to legend, a wealthy landlord, Duni Chand of the Patti village, had five daughters, all equally beautiful and talented. One day, he asked them: "Who provides you with food and shelter?"

Four of them replied – "Why you do father".

His fifth daughter, Rajni, replied, "No, it's God who provides all."

Enraged with her answer, Duni Chand marries Rajni to a leper and casts her out of the family to punish her and tells her, let's see if God will provide for you. She dutifully stands by her leper husband and takes him to Amritsar, a cultural center in the heart of Punjab.

She did odd chores to feed her husband and herself. It is said, Bibi Rajani placed her husband beneath the *Beri Tree*, as she struggled to carry him when he could no longer walk.

While she was gone, her husband watched as crows dipped in the lake and emerged pure white. He followed the crows' example and he grabbed hold of a low hanging branch from the *Beri Tree* to aid

148

his crawl to the Sarovar lake, submerging himself entirely except for one finger that he kept above the water.

When his wife returned after failing to secure help, she found her husband gone. Then a beautiful young man approached her, saying that he was her husband. She did not believe him. The man held up his finger still leprosy-ridden and said, "it's true, it is me – your husband. I am cured."

He relayed his story of the crows and his submergence into the lake and then she believed him. He was cured but his one finger served as a reminder and proof to his wife and others. He knew his wife would never believe him and that is why he left one finger above water. His faith and belief that the water could cure him after witnessing what happened to the crows was a huge factor in his miracle.

When Guru Ram Das Ji was informed of this miracle, he set about to develop the reservoir into a sacred bathing tank enjoyed by millions each year to this day. The tree was named Dukh Bhanjani – it means *eradicator of suffering.*

Legend has it that if you bathe where the tree touches the Sarovar lake, it will cleanse the mind and soul of sin and heal the body of ailments and disease.

Faith and belief are an incredible power on their own. Positive thinking alone promotes wellbeing, thus having a miraculous effect on our body and mind. We know this to be fact today in many areas of our life.

We have all heard modern-day stories of impossible cures by dying patients due to unconventional methods and so on. Myths or legends, facts or fiction – it is down to the individual to believe or not believe.

The veracity of the lepers claims to its healing power–for many, purely a matter of faith & belief.

A believer will relish its mystical powers and believe in its cures. A non-believer will be left sceptical and doubting. For me, it is an individual experience.

***

We visited the Golden Temple's Sarovar lake in the early hours, around one o'clock in the morning during the winter of 2014. Due to its popularity and over crowdedness, we wanted to experience it during a quiet and calm time. It turned out to be the best decision.

Before you could enter the Golden Temple, you have to remove your shoes and socks. At the entrance of the gates, there are running waterways that you must walk through *(the cleansing of feet)* as all feet must be clean on entering the sacred site.

Men and women must wear headscarves/turbans. You can purchase headscarves from local vendors outside the golden temple. My daughter and I wrapped up our hair, we removed our shoes at the gates and cleansed our feet before entering.

The temple is well guarded at all times. As we walked through the famous gates, we all gasped. The sheer beauty of the place was mesmerizing. A place of pilgrimage for many and curiosity by others. The temple conveyed a unique magical atmosphere at night. Sounds of prayers appeared enhanced and tranquility enshrouded us.

The temple is ringed by a marble walkway, the Golden Temple is donned in genuine gold that gleams brightly in the night. The moon's presence, bright and luminescent casts its magic all around. Singing from the holy book echoes through speakers as we strolled around.

I felt a spiritual calm take over me. It has been many years since the feeling of wonder captivated me the way it did that night. As we ambled around, I observed as adults walked into the lake, chanting prayers and lowering themselves further beneath the lake

150

before emerging, performing rituals while doing so. I was enchanted!

The whole atmosphere was surreal and magical to me. I watched my daughter as she took in the sights as we continued around the marble walkway. Her eyes lit up with wonder too. My husband, who is a spiritual man, was simply in his element.

We continued around the walkway until we neared the Famous Tree. I watched people perform rituals and pray. I followed the lead of our family guide until it was time to cleanse ourselves in the sacred lake.

I was so emersed in the spiritual experience and the deep emotions of those around me that I felt my whole inner being lifted.

We saw the steps leading down into the lake. I took my husband and daughter's hand and we walked. We went as far as we could manage with a five-year-old. The three of us stayed unmoving for a while. It was a surreal and magical moment to experience, one I shall never forget.

Several hours later, we were on the plane back to the United Kingdom, having spent three weeks in India. Half the time we were in Punjab and the other half in New Delhi. Now, this is where my story takes on a lead of its own.

Following our submergence into the Sacred Golden Temple Lake, as the months went by, my daughter's eczema lessened dramatically until its severity disappeared. Within eighteen months, it remained a distant memory. She had the occasional slight flair up, as if something wanted to remind us of what water can do. Her asthma greatly improved, too. She hasn't had a hospital visit since.

I can almost hear the sceptics – *this could simply be explained: a child grows out of her childhood aliments as all kids do. Or maybe it could have been a short-term less severe medical condition which had lasted years.*

But the sudden dramatic reduction in the months that followed have me leaning towards other possibilities such as the spiritual dominances of that sacred water. A child cannot grow out of a log-term aliment so quickly.

Since our visit to the Golden Temple Lake, my daughter has not suffered the severity of harsh and painful outbreaks that she did prior to entering that water. I wanted it to work so much that I believed it would heal her, and it did.

Once in the temple my belief was so convincing that I was enveloped by an unexplainable euphoria of spiritual calmness.

Faith and confidence — those positive vibes I sent out into the universe — the *law of attraction* worked magic. No one can explain the unexplained.

Mine is just one true magical and mystical story. There are hundreds and thousands of healing stories which rise from the power of water. Myth or legend, believer or not – The Sacred Sarovar Lake is enchanting, and I for one strongly believe that a miracle happened to us while the waters of the Golden Temple held us in her brace.

The Golden Temple with its Sacred Lake feeds over 40,000 people a day. Each person who enters the temple is fed a substantial meal of dahl and chapattis. It is a place of pilgrimage visited by millions each year.

Volunteers feed everyone who offer up their time, with no recompense. They believe it is an honour to serve the Temple.

Each person who passes through the gates are treated the same, whether king or pauper. In the main dining hall you all sit together.

No one is given special treatment. But when you enter that lake, you feel that *Nature* baptizes you with water.

152

D.G.'s bio:

 **D.G. Torrens** is a UK and USA bestselling Author/Poet and a founding member of Bestsellingreads.com and Authorcityuk. D.G. has written and published 20 books to date. A prolific writer with a deep passion for the written word. Her first book, (memoirs) *Amelia's Story*, has inspired people the world over and has been downloaded over 500k times worldwide. Amelia's Story is the author's true-life story. It was never intended for publication.

The author then went on to write military romance, romantic suspense, romantic drama, contemporary romance novels and poetry books, which have been received well.

The success of Amelia's Story led the author to over 65 radio appearances including the BBC RADIO WM 95.6 FM, in 2014/15 on the Adrian Goldberg breakfast show, where she lent her time as a weekly Headline Reviewer for 12 months.

Following on from the BBC Radio, D.G has since been interviewed by, Award-Winning Radio DJ, Graham Torrington on the late-night show at BBC Radio WM and David Driver Author & DJ at Drystone Radio FM as well as by American Radio Host/author/actor, Cyrus Webb at CoversationsLive.com Radio for Mississippi.

https://www.facebook.com/dgtorrens

A LOVE LETTER TO WATER

David Zetland (author, economist), THE NETHERLANDS

As a child, I was afraid of swimming due to a bad experience at a swimming lesson. I was about five years old and not sure about water — let alone holding my breath under water. The instructor was not patient. She pushed my head under and I was drowning. After that "lesson", I stayed away from water. I didn't want to drown.

A few years later in summer camp, I met another swim instructor. Mark took an interest in me and my fear. He told me "you can rest when you want — the pool's edge isn't far". His obvious advice allayed my fear. Soon, I was swimming over the deep end, unworried even if my feet couldn't touch the bottom. The edge was never far away. That summer, I was awarded "most improved swimmer".

In high school, I was on the swim team and played water polo. I was not fast, but I swam from edge to edge. I swallowed a lot of water as teammates crashed by, but I did not panic.

During university, I worked for one summer in Hawaii. Everyday, I swam in the sea, from one end of the cove to the other. The water was a bit murky. I couldn't see — let alone touch — the bottom, but the edge — the shore — was always there, just to the side.

One time the shadow of a fish (a shark?!) got between me and the shore. My heart hit 200 beats as I tried to levitate above the water. Luckily, the fish (a shark?!) had other intentions, and I made it home.

Over the years, I have swum, sailed, dived, and floated in pools, lakes, and seas all over the world — probably in thirty or more countries. I am so happy that I can swim. I am thankful that Mark took the time to help me trust myself in water. Water deserves our respect, but it is also a comforting, flowing, cooling companion.

Today, I teach students about the political-economy of water, its value in our lives, and the many ways we (mis)manage it. I do not teach about the joys of swimming, sailing, diving or floating in water. Those feelings cannot be taught. They must be experienced.

As an adult, I admire, respect and love water. I wish that others felt as strongly as I do about this precious, live-giving, life-affirming resource, but often they do not. A pity for them, a pity for us, a pity for our humanity and civilization.

I love water. It's an everyday miracle that deserves our appreciation and respect.

David's Bio:

David Zetland is a university lecturer at Leiden University College, where he teaches classes on economics, sustainability and entrepreneurship. He received his PhD in Agricultural Resource Economics from UC Davis, holds a Postdoctorate Fellowship in Natural Resource Economics and Political Economy at UC Berkleley, and served as a Senior Water Economist at Wageningen University. He also taught at Simon Fraser University in Vancouver, Canada. He actively blogs and has written three books: *The End of Abundance: economic solutions to water scarcity, Living with Water Scarcity,* and *The Best of Aguanomics.* David lives in Amsterdam.

WATER PRAYER

Giselle World (singer, healer), USA

We pray for the water

We pray for the healing of the water

Of all the waters,

The waters in the rivers, the oceans, the seas, the lakes all over the world

Understanding and honouring that it's all one great water

We pray for humanity to wake up and rise up to protect and preserve the sacredness of this precious element of water

Praying humanity can understand that the water inside of us is also precious and sacred.

To serve the Mother, our Great Mother, the Mother Earth is to serve ourselves.

We pray for rain, cleansing rain, aguita bendita llega a las tierras secas, bless the lands needing you.

Heal and bless our lungs—The Amazon, and all the forests, jungles and natural lands helping sustain us.

We are united in this prayer. We are visionaries and we can see a chance for the healing of this earth and it's water for future generations.

Gracias agüita. Thank you water. I love you water.

And so it is. Aho. Haux Haux.

Giselle bio:

Flutist and vocalist, Giselle is a captivating performing artist, who infuses ritual and indigenous culture into the electronic scene.

She is a classically trained musician, who has been journeying in the electronic music scene for over 10 years. Through her travels and love of ceremony, she's created a soundscape of unique, conscious textures and fusion of tribal electronic medicine music while curating an alchemic experience honouring the elements and inspiring healing through the powerful use of indigenous chants and ancient mantras.

She has been extensively in service to plant medicines, and an advocate for indigenous rights, as well as sharing about indigenous wisdom and culture all over the world using music as the main tool by teaching about the cultures through workshops and song circles. www.giselle.world

Water as fog at the top of Volcán Barú,
Chiriqui Province, Panama
(photo taken by Claudiu Murgan)

157

Manor House
905-648-4797
www.manor-house-publishing.com